THE *Lie* THAT BINDS

THE LIE THAT BINDS
Overcoming the Tragic Effects of Child Abuse

ISBN: 978-0-924748-89-9
UPC: 88571300059-8

Printed in the United States of America
© 2008 by Larry Sault and Clara Y. Heath

Milestones International Publishers
140 Danika Drive NW
Huntsville, AL 35806
(256) 830-0362; Fax (256) 830-9206
www.milestonesintl.com

Cover design by: Thirty Thumbs Design Works

1 2 3 4 5 6 7 8 9 10 11 / 09 08 07 06 05 04

THE *Lie* THAT BINDS

OVERCOMING THE TRAGIC
EFFECTS OF CHILD ABUSE

LARRY SAULT
AND
CLARA Y. HEATH

MILESTONES
INTERNATIONAL PUBLISHERS

DEDICATION

While contemplating this book, we have always tried to remain focused on why we chose, after all these years, to speak now, re-entering our prison of dirty secrets. We came to realize that, although there are many more reasons, three readily come to mind:

Eugene Wayne (Fats) Sault (1959-1988)
Arthur Charles (Charlie) Sault (1957-1999)
Garry (Brooksey) Sault (1954-2003)

Although it has been a few years now, it seemed like just yesterday when we shared secrets and dreamed our dreams of moving mountains together. Who would have known at the time that these guys would not see the fulfillment of the words we spoke? Who would have known that their journey on this earth would be cut short and they would make the transition to the spirit world so soon? Death certainly was not part of the plan, even though in those early years it seemed like we were born to lose, to swim up river, to run against the wind.

Like all of us, our brothers had both good and bad qualities that shaped their world from our earliest years. Fats, was a quick thinker. He had a very good sense of humor. At his darkest hour, he could laugh and joke. Deep within, he was tender, passionate, and at various times expressed those qualities.

On the flip side, he could be very violent, even to the point of being filled with rage. A rage that, mixed with alcohol, would eventually take him to the State Penitentiary for four solid years. A rage that would become part of the final chapter of his life.

Prior to his death he talked about the dream of knowing what it was to experience peace, build his marriage relationship, raise his family, own his own home, drive a nice car, and yes, even becoming a confident leader within the community. Some of these things he did see, while others he was still working on at the time of his death. The point is, regardless of his situation, he had a dream. A dream that was cut short because of his own beliefs and choices!

Charlie also had a sense of humor, but deep down he was a shy and very mediocre guy. He was talented, very meticulous, and very clean (when he was sober). He loved music, particularly Elvis Presley. He often imitated Elvis by trying to sing his tunes. He was a very likeable guy.

Like the rest of us, his addiction to alcohol started early and led eventually to his first car accident, one that claimed the lives of others and left him unconscious for at least three months in the intensive care unit. Through much prayer and months of medical attention, he survived, was released, and began making his journey to recovery.

Unfortunately, it didn't take long before he went back to the lifestyle he was accustomed to before the accident. As time past and foolishness once again took its grip on him, he would find himself in yet another car wreck. This time it was not as severe, though nonetheless traumatizing for family members. His addiction to alcohol ultimately brought him to a place of drifting across the country, not caring what he looked like, smelled like, or what others thought of him. Over the years of his alcoholism, Charlie spent time in prison for various offences and at his release would talk about wanting to go straight and get his life in order. His dreams and aspirations were cut short when in August of 1999 a third car accident ultimately claimed his life.

Garry was a twin brother to Larry. They were probably closer than any other family members and total opposites. Garry was not a fighter, but had a soft and gentle heart. In many ways, he was like our Uncle Joe.

He had a tendency to follow his twin, but only so far. They left home and moved to Toronto together, worked construction, and even took on the challenge of driving 18-wheelers together. We remember him for his mastery at playing the guitar and banjo, and his ability to manhandle and maneuver the big rigs.

It seemed that his personality was a magnet for abusive people to be drawn to him. He found himself surrounded by strangers he thought were his friends. He would often talk about how people treated him, shafted him, and always seemed to take advantage of him, yet he would not stand up until he was pushed against the wall. It would seem that destructive associations had redirected his path, even though he too had verbalized the life he dreamed of living.

Sexual abuse in his youth played a major role in his failed marriage and sexual preference. It upset his work ethic and ultimately ended his life through the disease called AIDS. Through all his torment about an angry God, on his death bed, as our sister remembers, he made his amends with God, others, and even our parents.

It is because of these guys that we write. It is because of these guys that we are more determined than ever before to pursue our dreams and accomplish what we can while we have breath. These three brothers helped shape our lives and instilled a determination in us, whether they knew it or not – a determination to fulfill that which we believe the Creator put us here to accomplish.

We dedicate this book to these three brothers who made the journey to the spirit world before us and now root us on to finish the race that was set before the Sault family.

ACKNOWLEDGMENTS

Any story sounds true until someone tells the other side and sets the record straight.

The Lie that Binds is our experience, and we tell it, not from hearts of bitterness or malice, but from hearts of courage and hope.

Hope that those who have suffered in similar ways would become courageous enough to stand up and deal with their own past and move on to fulfilling their lifelong dreams.

This book could not have been written without the rich relationships we've shared with so many people who have encouraged us to tell the truth. Many of you have helped us in the development of ideas, breathing clarity into situations at critical junctures of our journey to wellness.

We thank our siblings and our mother who have supported the idea of setting the record straight, knowing that you too, have a story, which could in fact be, the other side!

Oftentimes we heard it said, "When the student is ready, the teacher appears." Dr. Jim Richards has not only been that teacher, but a friend and advisor. Thank you, Doc, for helping us bring this book to reality.

No one could have been more fortunate than Claire Heath and Larry Sault to have worked for such a dynamic and wise gentleman as Mr. Donald P. Kennedy; First American Corporation. Thank you Mr. Kennedy, for believing in us, and our vision to reach out and help others.

Last but not least, we thank our spouses, Sonya Sault, and Garry Heath. You've been with us, in the good times and the bad. You know us better than anyone and yet you stood with us and supported us in the desire to help others see what they already know. The Truth.

TABLE OF CONTENTS

INTRODUCTION

Our dad confessed Jesus Christ as his personal Lord and Savior in a Pentecostal church service in 1957, but that didn't stop him from having his way with our family. There didn't seem to be much positive change taking place in the home, except that our regular dose of domestic abuse was now accompanied by a steady helping of religion. To say it was a confusing time would be something of an understatement. On the one hand, we began going to church and hearing about God on a regular basis. On the other, our living situation was in some ways continuing to get worse by the day.

But already we're getting ahead of ourselves. Let us take you back to the early years of our family, to shine a light on the experiences that set our foundation for life, such as it was.

If we had to put a word to the conditions in which we grew up, it would have to be "difficult." Or "brutal." While there are a few qualities we picked up from our parents that we're grateful for today, the truth is that they did a lot of damage and inflicted a great deal of pain. As we've moved on with our lives, had our own families, and sought healing and deliverance from our Father in heaven, we've come across a multitude of people who can identity in one way or another with our own series of challenges and life experiences. God forbid, but you may be one of them. If that's the case, this book has been written and uniquely presented so that you can cast aside the shame, confusion, and anger that may continue to fester on the inside.

Now is the time to expose those inner demons. Healing and a lifetime free of torment are closer than you might think.

CHAPTER ONE

The Hand of Violence

LARRY 1955-1981

As far back as I can remember, our family was nomadic, moving frequently from one place to another on our home reservation, going wherever we needed to go to make sure there was a roof over our heads. When I was just a child, in the 1950s, my great-uncle gave my father fifty acres of land on Mississaugas of New Credit First Nation Reservation in southern Ontario. Half of that property was occupied with forest while the other half contained land suitable for farming. We were going to need both kinds of land, because the farm was going to make us money while the bush was going to provide wood to keep us warm during the winter. While most people today take heat for granted, the only ways for my brothers and sisters and I to stay warm in the house we grew up in was to get close to the oil-burning lamps or keep feeding the wood stove. Feeding the stove meant we had to cut a lot of wood, which was always a terrible burden, but in the coldest months was truly miserable.

My dad started building a new house in the fall of 1957, though it was almost two years from the time of construction before it was ready to move into. It had two levels, with a kitchen, living room, and master bedroom on the main floor and four rooms upstairs that went unfinished for years. There wasn't any running water and quarters were cramped. Though there were only six of us kids in 1959, within a few years our numbers exploded to sixteen. Instead of living with us, my grandfather stayed in a small shanty located fifty feet in front of the house.

Building the house promised to be a long ordeal from the beginning, made longer by the fact that my dad broke his arm working construction in Niagara Falls that year. I don't recall exactly how it happened, but he fell off the side of a dump truck. That certainly wasn't the strangest thing to ever happen to him, though. When the drinking started, he became unpredictable. The only thing predictable about it was that people were going to get hurt, and those people almost always included the kids.

It wasn't just the hard work that comes to mind when I go back to those earliest days; it was the violence.

My earliest memories involve watching my dad, with one hand in a sling, digging out the new house's basement with my oldest brother. He was no more than a child at the time himself, but he was nonetheless responsible for operating the tractor as my dad and mother maneuvered the scoop that was in tow. As I've said, it wasn't just the hard work that comes to mind when I go back to those earliest days; it was the violence. My dad was always angry and on edge, which meant we all had to walk on eggshells when we were around him. My brother got cuffed around a lot during the house's construction, even for the slightest infraction … maybe even for no infraction at all, but that was the volatile man my father was.

Glimpses into the outside world were rare.

When we finally moved into the house, I remember watching television for the first time. It was a small black and white unit, but it was a big deal since it offered us our first real exposure to the outside world. Glimpses into the outside world were rare back then. Growing up on the reservation was often a very isolating experience, as I was eventually going to learn the hard way.

Our farming days started with the construction of an old makeshift barn. My dad bought a couple of cows to go with it. As the farm grew, the workload for the boys – there were three of us then – gradually increased until we were working most of the day. There were a lot of other kids on the reservation whose parents didn't make them work nearly as much, and I disdained them for the fact that they seemed to be enjoying their childhood while we were being robbed of ours. In my view, they seemed to get away with doing next to nothing while we worked some days from first light to sunset.

There was nothing fair about it. The girls did all the household chores while the boys ran the farm, which involved a lot of work. We cleaned the stables, milked the cows twice a day, fed the cows, baled hay, cut the grain, and planted the seed. Everything that farmers do, we did it all on our own. The burden of responsibility was far greater than anything we saw in other kids on the reservation.

Looking back today, I can say that my own children never, ever experienced that kind of heavy labor.

School was not a priority in our home. It wasn't valued at all.

In addition to maintaining the farm, we cut what seemed like an endless supply of wood. My dad received a government contract to provide most of the Native people that were on welfare on our reservation – a substantial number– with firewood. We were cutting wood in the bush for hours every day, a chore that was completely disproportionate to all our other work. We had to start early almost every morning, and it was common for us to stay home from school in order to fill the quotas. The woodcutting went on throughout the weekends in the freezing temperatures of Canadian winter, and started immediately after school on the days we were allowed to go. When we weren't cutting it, we were delivering it.

Frankly, school was not a priority in our home. It wasn't valued at all. My father used to say, "I only made it to second grade, and I've already forgotten more stuff than any of you kids will ever know!" Unfortunately, that was his stance on modern education. When I was a young boy, I distinctly recall wanting to be either a professional baseball player or a medical doctor. With the amount of schooling we were allowed, and the constant distraction of our father's abuse, I never had much of a chance.

If it had just been the work, I might have been okay with it, but each and every day was full of inescapable violence. That was my father's method of controlling us. He didn't seem to know of any better way, and we suffered the consequences. If our dad called us to get up in the morning, we had to jump to attention and do what he told us to … or else! If I were to sleep for even a few extra minutes, he would grab me and throw me out of bed. Violence was the only reality we knew, and fear was our way of life.

We weren't sons and daughters in my eyes. There was a sense of disciplined order to the way life was conducted, as though we were an army. In all honesty, we were slaves, and we were treated as such. My brothers and I didn't even feel like we were part of a family most of the time, and though my dad may have had a compassionate moment every once in a long while, we rarely saw his lighter side, the natural right-heartedness of a father.

We weren't sons and daughters in my eyes.

I remember one occasion when my mother took all the kids and left our dad, bringing us with her to our grandmother's house to stay for a while. I don't recall whether this was before or after his salvation, because my dad's binge drinking was a constant factor in our lives, but we all walked ten miles to get away from him. He was a mean drunk. When we got to our grandmother's, she wasn't very hospitable. My mom's mother always seemed to be as cold as ice, with an almost constant scowl on her face. In retrospect, it seems as though she didn't want anything to do with her own grandchildren.

Even though this is a specific event I remember, it wasn't out of the ordinary. My parents fought constantly, and these fights usually ended with my dad beating my mother. But when my dad's temper was turned on any of the kids, she never stood up for us.

I hated my dad. I realize that those are strong words, but I really did hate him with all of my heart. This is an issue I've dealt with since changing the direction of my life, but at the time I often thought about killing him. That's how strong my hatred for him was. Considering how violent our everyday world had become, it's not surprising that our violence was occasionally turned back on him.

My father and grandfather found ways to try to turn our hatred and the violence we felt toward them on each other. They taught us how to fight, and my dad even built a boxing ring in our yard to facilitate the fights. He made us older boys put boxing gloves on and hit each other. Even when we didn't want to fight, he wouldn't let us give up. Eventually, it got to the point where we had to draw blood from our opponent, our own brothers.

My dad got his kicks by inviting his own brothers over to watch us go at it. We didn't want to participate in that violence against each other, but it was never about what we did or didn't want to do. It was all about force, the force our dad exerted on us to get what he wanted. Despite this, the boys were reasonably close. The old saying must be true, that the enemy of my enemy is my friend, because we found ourselves united in our hatred for our dad. That said, I don't think we had an appreciation for what real closeness was.

Between the two men of the house, there was no escaping their cruelty.

As easy as it would be to blame my dad for all the hurts I experienced under his rule, some of the fault has to be shared by my grandfather, who had just as much a hand in the violence of our home as my dad did. My father told us how he grew up without a mother, and considering how mean and miserable my grandfather was, it's easy to understand how my dad turned out the way he did. I don't know whatever happened to my grandfather, whether he was always mean or if it got worse after the death of our grandmother, but he ruled the family with an iron fist as well. Between the two men of the house, there was no escaping their cruelty.

In the early 1960s, our dad joined the Ironworkers. As a tradesman, he spent longer and longer periods away from the family, and nobody complained about the extended absences. For over ten years, he lived and worked in Detroit during the week, coming home only on weekends. Because there wasn't a lot of work available in our region, this weekly migration was pretty common for Natives. They traveled where the work was, working throughout the summers and drawing unemployment during the winters.

The weeks when he was gone were wonderful. It was like we could breathe a sigh of relief, not having to walk on pins and needles anymore. For years, Fridays were filled with expectant waiting, wondering when he would be home and what mood he would be in. It certainly didn't much help matters when our mother would get frustrated and fear monger us by warning us about his impending arrival. "You're going to get it when he gets home," she would say. Without fail, his presence on the weekends brought with it heightened tension. In modern language, he would be described as a toxic presence, to put it mildly.

The continual violence was bad enough on its own, but when it was partnered with religion, the situation became infinitely more confusing and damaging. For example, both our father and grandfather manipulated Scripture to their own advantage, to pound us into submission. When our dad would discipline us, often for no tangible reason, he would spout off a verse, such as Proverbs 22:6: Train up a child in the way he should go: and when he is old, he will not depart from it (KJV). Then he would wail on us, hitting us with anything he could get his hands on. He would use the Bible as his

21

own personal excuse to get away with abuse. Honour thy father and thy mother: that thy days may be long upon the land which the Lord thy God giveth thee (Exodus 20:12, KJV). By the time I was 14, I'd had enough and wasn't going to put up with that anymore. But after a while these verses became seriously engrained in my heart to the point that I couldn't even talk about our parents for fear that I would be dishonoring them. We couldn't stand up for ourselves.

We felt deeply conflicted during those years, on one hand because we knew that what they were doing was wrong, and yet there was an instilling of Pentecostal fear in us. Every day we had it drilled into us that the consequence for failing to entertain every one of our parents' whims was that we were going straight to hell. They were fear mongering with the Word of God, which really messed with our heads. There came a time when something inside me snapped, and I decided that if I was going to go to hell, then I was going to do it good.

The continual violence was bad enough on its own, but when it was partnered with religion, the situation became infinitely more confusing.

The Pentecostal church we attended was one of the most lively on our reservation, and our dad insisted that we become a part of it. To that end, we became family singers, forming two quartets, one for the boys and another for the girls. My dad played the guitar while the rest of us provided vocal accompaniment. I can guarantee that participation wasn't voluntary. Just like everything else in our lives, we were forced into it. Speaking for the oldest boys, none of us wanted to sing, certainly not in public. If we didn't, our dad gave us a certain look that told us all we needed to know, that when we left church we were in for a beating. So while we were in front of the congregation, we put on a show.

Thus began our singing careers, short lived though they were. My dad even went so far as to take us on the road, traveling to different churches and religious functions. He stood up before the church and did the religious song and dance, declaring how much he loved the Lord and how much his life had changed since finding Jesus. What the churchgoers didn't know was that just before we'd walked inside, he had been slapping us around.

Throughout all this, our family was desperately poor, but I didn't know it. Without anything to compare it to, I assumed that the way we lived was the standard. I didn't know what poor was because our parents controlled the money so carefully that we never saw a penny of it. To them, we were little more than a workforce to exploit.

In addition to our regular workload, we spent our summers in a nearby strawberry farm that belonged to a family that our parents had befriended. Every spring, we labored by picking berries, cucumbers, tomatoes, peppers, apples, grapes, peaches, and anything else that the local farmers had growing. By the time fall came, we were working in the tobacco fields. The entire summer was spent outside gathering the harvests, work which in turn supplied everything we needed to live. And a little extra.

Each and every member of my family... became financial train wrecks when we left home for.

As far as what money we actually earned, that's another thing we never knew. Our parents didn't give us our own money. Because of this, as we got older, none of us knew how to handle money when we had it. Each and every member of my family, myself included, became financial train wrecks when we left home for the first time, and these troubles can all be attributed to the unceasing control our parents exercised over the family's income. When I finally had my first job outside the home and started earning money, I blew every cent, not even thinking about rent and that paying it had to be a priority. I faced eviction after eviction, instead preoccupying my income on alcohol and living hand to mouth.

Physical abuse wasn't the extent of our suffering as children. My dad picked on us mercilessly. "You guys are no good," he would tell us. "You're filthy, lazy, and you'll never be anything. Just wait and see, you won't amount to nothing!" The sad truth is that these words had profound effects on us. Most of my siblings are living out those words today.

Work was never pleasurable for us, so when we were old enough to make our own decisions about work, we chose to avoid the very thing that would help us maintain a livelihood. My heart still breaks today because I witness family members living out the very words spoken over us.

Something inside me just didn't accept it the way my siblings did. Because of my anger and my strong personality, I resisted it. There was a hard part of me that said, "You just watch, buddy. I am going to amount to something, and I'll prove to you that I am somebody." And sure enough, that attitude propelled me to great things.

What I didn't fully grasp when I was growing up was why I behaved the way I did. I was more than a product of my upbringing. I had leadership qualities that, at least in the beginning, only manifested as anger. Even as a kid in grade school, the other children would follow me. We had a teacher who would lock the class outside in the rain during lunch breaks and not open the doors again until the bell rang. We would be standing outside in the pouring rain, knocking on the door, and be waiting there for an entire hour. One day, I complained about this to my dad, and he looked me right in the eyes and said, "If she does that again, you bring these kids home."

I had leadership qualities that, at least in the beginning, only manifested as anger.

The next time it happened, I gathered my classmates together, which included some of my cousins and other relatives. Instead of taking them back to our house, we went to my uncle's house where we went inside to wait out the storm. We sat around and ate cookies, which made me feel like a real hero. Chances are I wouldn't have felt so good about myself if I'd known what was coming.

Unfortunately for us, my dad came to pick us up at school that afternoon and some girl ratted on us, telling him that we ran away from school for the afternoon and had just came back to catch the bus. When I got home from school that day, my dad gave me the beating of my life. I couldn't believe what was happening. The very thing he had told me to do was what I was being punished for. I looked to my mother for some help, but instead she was standing nearby egging my dad on, encouraging him to beat me harder! "Hit him again!" she cried. "He thinks he's so smart, hit him! Hit him some more!"

Inside, I snapped that day. All I was guilty of was exercising my natural leadership abilities. The kids at school gravitated toward me, following me in any group situation. As we got older, I became more and more of a hero among my peers. I was mastering the art of fighting in hand-to-hand combat, so people started to look up to me at a young age. Of course, those same tendencies later put me in prison, but at the time I couldn't see past my own fists.

Another thing that started as a kid that eventually got me in trouble with the law was theft. As we got older, we were supporting the younger kids, and the best way for us to do that was to steal from our parents. After they would go shopping, we would go into the cupboards and take things for ourselves, knowing we might never see it again if we didn't. We'd take cans of fruit or treats or bread, anything we could get our hands on, and then stash it for later. If we were ever accused of stealing by our parents, we would blame each other. And sometimes, for instance if my brother took something and I didn't want to see him get beat, I would step in and take the blame in order to protect him.

I will never forget the series of events that finally led me to make the decision to go. Everything I had learned so far about God told me that if I stood up to my dad, I would end up going to hell, so I decided to embrace that destiny wholeheartedly.

I had an older sister that my mother was always against, for some reason I still don't know. They didn't have a relationship back then, and they still don't to this day, even though she has tried to establish one again and again. One morning, my dad told us that we weren't going to school that day. The two of us stood our ground and told him there wasn't any question about it, we were going no matter what he said. My dad reacted immediately, rushing forward to attack us. As I remember it, he wasn't coming at me so much as at her, since she'd been the one mouthing off to him. We were standing at the top of the stairs when he started coming up, so I stepped in to protect her. I swung at him with everything I had and suckered him right in the face.

As he whaled on me, I retreated into myself and told myself, "It's fine. My day's coming.

Strange though it may sound, that was probably one of the best things that had happened in my life to that point. At fourteen, I was done taking his crap and I was finally going to start fighting back. Well, despite my efforts, I took a beating that day. After all, he was six feet tall and two hundred fifty pounds. As he whaled on me, I retreated into myself and told myself, "It's fine. My day's coming. You'll get yours. Just wait your turn."

About two weeks later, my twin brother Garry and I were in the bush cutting wood with my dad. It was early in the morning and my dad was angry, as usual. In the heat of the moment, he picked up a piece of wood and hit my brother with it. Immediately I saw my opportunity to step in and give my dad the payback he so richly deserved. I cursed him with every word I knew, picked up a club of my own and pointed it at him. I called to Garry, telling him to get behind me. "Cut your own wood!" I shouted at my dad. "We're done here!"

I made sure to keep an eye on him the whole time as we walked out of the bush that day. He was as mad as I had ever seen him, and I wasn't planning to turn my back on him ever again. If he came at us, I was prepared to do anything to make sure he didn't hurt us again, but he let us go.

My brother Garry was a passive guy, unlike me. I would fly off the handle in a second given the chance, a trait I knew I had inherited from my dad. We had both contemplated leaving many times, but for the longest time it was just talk. As that day wore on, I made it clear to him that I was planning on getting off the farm by the end of the day, whether he came with me or not. Of course, I was hoping he would come along.

He tried talking me out of it. "What are you going to do?" he asked me. "Where are you going to go?" But I already had a plan in place. Toronto wasn't too far away, and it was a big city. I knew I would survive and make a life for myself, but I didn't have a specific place to go. Garry was afraid and even though he had clung to my coattails our entire lives, he had doubts that we would be able to make it on our own.

I packed my bags that day, getting ready what few possessions I had. When my dad saw what I was doing, he merely shrugged. "If you think you can make it on your own, boy, there's the road," he said. Because he was the kind of guy that tried to manipulate us by putting fear into us, he just sat down at the bottom of the stairs and read the paper while I packed. His reason for doing it was clear: the only way out the door was down the stairs, right past where he was waiting. There would be no escaping without him knowing.

When it was time to go, Garry stayed upstairs. I slung my bag over my shoulder and walked down, straight past my dad without saying a word. I walked right out the door without looking back.

Garry was watching from the upstairs window of the house, still hoping I wasn't going to go through with it. He called out to me to stay, but instead I turned around and shouted up to him. "If you're coming with me, that's fine. If you're not, that's fine too." With that, I turned around again and kept walking. I hadn't made it even halfway to the road when I heard his voice behind me. "Just a minute, I'm coming too."

We left the house on a Friday, but didn't have anywhere to go until the following Monday, so we spent the weekend in the old barn where we were storing hay. I think my dad thought I was thinking twice about leaving. Even Garry thought I had changed my mind, that I was finally listening to reason, but in reality I was just waiting to put all the pieces together. One of our neighbors on the reservation had given me a lead on a possible job in Toronto.

When Monday came, my twin brother and I left the reservation and headed for the big city of Toronto. Our first stop was the labor pool office that our neighbor had told us about. My brother didn't have the first clue about what to say or what to do, so I quieted him down and said, "Just let me do all the talking and everything's going to work out."

Before we went inside, we had one more hurdle to overcome: social insurance numbers. I didn't know anything about the subject, so I had to ask someone how many digits were in a social insurance number. When I found out there were nine, I just made up nine numbers and scribbled them down on a paper. When we went in, we said we were old enough to work and gave them our made-up numbers. Since government offices didn't have computers yet in those days, we got away with it. Nobody even checked to see whether or not we were legit.

Within the day, we had jobs at an old glove factory in the city. It wasn't much, but at least it was a paying job. Our first salary was $85 a week, which may not seem like much now, but at the time it was pretty good money. Especially seeing as we were just barely fifteen years old and were lying about our age.

Even though our pay was good by the standards of the day, we still had to subsidize it with stealing. We stole men's clothes, shoes, jackets, all kinds of stuff. You name it, we were stealing it, usually from department stores. Our name for those stores was "boosters," a tongue in cheek reference, because they helped us boost our pay. We didn't always get away it, though, and sometimes I got caught. It was pure humiliation when that happened, as if we weren't living with enough shame already, because my name would be in the local paper for stealing and getting into fights with security guards. We could brush it off by laughing about it and getting drunk, but deep down the shame was hard to live with.

I was completely driven by my will to make it in the real world and prove my dad wrong. The last thing I was going to do was return to the reservation with my hat in my hand, so I resolved not to go back, even for a visit, for at least six months – a goal I had no trouble meeting.

I was completely driven by my will to make it in the real world and prove my dad wrong.

Eventually, we started coming home on weekends, and that's when I first got into trouble with alcohol. It's true that I had done my share of drinking in the past, but in the environment of the reserve where all our friends drank for days straight, sniffed gas, and took drugs, I found myself on a slippery slope. First, we drank heavily, but just on Friday nights. Before long, entire weekends were being consumed. It got to the point where I stopped caring, drinking steadily for several days at a time. Days soon turned to weeks, and before I knew what was happening, I would beg, borrow, and steal to get my habit looked after.

After a year of going back and forth between Toronto and the reserve, I decided to head further south and live in the States. By this time, Garry had apparently had his fill and chose not to come with me, instead moving back home. While I occasionally stayed over for a night or two at my parents' house, going back on a permanent basis simply wasn't an option for me. One of my buddies knew someone who worked in Rochester, New York at a hot tar roofing company, so that seemed as good a place as any to start up again.

With nobody to keep me in line, that's where my alcoholism finally took hold. The bars in Rochester were open far later than in Ontario, as late as 3:00 in the morning on weeknights. I tried to pay my rent first, but every last cent left went to booze. Though I had come to work, I ended up partying the whole year. At the age of sixteen, I was completely hooked on alcohol.

At the age of sixteen, I was completely hooked on alcohol.

By the time of my year in Rochester, the Vietnam War was in full swing, and I came to the conclusion that the best thing for me was to enlist in the United States Army. I would have gone, too, were it not for the pull of alcohol. I don't think I was ever able to keep my head clear enough to make a firm decision on the subject, so instead of shipping overseas, I made my way back to my home reserve.

In 1970, I joined the Ironworkers, just as my father had done before me. The work was hard, but the pay was the best I had ever had, $3.85 per hour. The worst part of the arrangement was the union company I was keeping. The union was comprised of a pretty rough, ragtag crowd, and together with them I traveled to jobs all over the place. As an Ironworker, we had international status and didn't need papers to cross back and forth over the border, so we went wherever the work took us.

The drinking was starting to take its toll on me. After a few drinks, it was easy to find myself in violent situations. It didn't take much to wake up one morning and find myself in jail for getting impaired, robbing somebody, and beating them senseless. Things were going from bad to worse, with no end in sight.

That is, until I met Sonya one weekend at a bar in Brantford, Ontario.

Actually, we had already met on the reservation when we attended elementary school together. Sonya had been in the eighth grade and I was in seventh. I had always had a crush on her, feelings I had managed to keep hidden from her. Secretly, I had wanted to marry her, and seeing her now brought all those same emotions rushing back up to the surface.

Sonya had grown up in a home near mine. Like a lot of people on the reservation, her father used to drink a lot on weekends, but he was never, ever violent to his family. Even when he was three sheets to the wind, he was still soft and tender to those he cared about. Unlike my own dad, he treated his kids like gold. Because of this, she didn't see alcohol as being a problem. As soon as she got to know me better, and the effects alcohol had on my behavior, she was blown away by the degree to which alcoholism had taken over my life. Of course, I didn't think I had a problem. As far as I was concerned, I was just like everybody else ... in denial.

Despite my problems, we started a relationship. Within a year, we were living together. In 1972, we got married. Unfortunately, nothing in life had prepared me, or her, for what a marriage relationship was going to be like. Sure enough, I quickly turned into my father. He was the only role model I had.

As far as I was concerned, I was just like everybody else ... in denial.

Even though I loved Sonya, I continued seeing other women after we were married. I didn't see sexual promiscuity as being a problem, having witnessed my dad do it his entire life. Drinking and having as much sex as possible as often as I could get it, that's what I thought life was all about.

My lifestyle led me down some dark paths. Basically, I didn't stop drinking. Ever. In the first five years of my marriage, I was in and out of prison, serving terms lasting anywhere from a few days to a few months. Instead of calming down, my behavior was becoming more and more erratic. Sonya was having to call the police on me continually because when I lost control, which was often, I would beat her up. I was falling into our family's pattern without much of a fight.

The only difference was that Sonya didn't put up with me the way my mom had put up with my dad. It made me angry a lot of the time, since I still had it drilled into me from my religious indoctrination that women were supposed to submit to their husbands. In one incident, when we were visiting Sonya's family, she said something that made me mad, and I started to physically attack her. Right in front of her parents! Well, I stunned them. They couldn't believe what they were seeing. In my rage, I remember shoving Sonya into a wall and cuffing her in the face. Her parents hadn't raised their kids in a violent home and I felt they didn't know how to respond to me. They didn't know what to do.

My father-in-law didn't say a word to me that night. That's the way he was, but you can be sure he took up the subject with Sonya another time when I wasn't around. "Divorce this guy," he finally told her. "Divorce this guy or he's going to kill you one day." When I think back to that experience, I'm filled with embarrassment that events had spiraled to that point. One of the things I'm most grateful for is that my father-in-law lived to see the day that I transformed myself into a peaceful, loving husband and father.

But that was still years away. By 1978, Sonya and I had been married for six years, and every day had gotten successively worse than the one before. My drinking binges were lasting several months at a time and I was completely unable to take care of my family. Sonya was surviving on her government allowance and I would show up at the house every few days to steal things that I could sell to support my alcoholism.

I contemplated suicide more times than I could count. I never acted on it, but it was a possibility that I considered just about every day.

It's hard to believe, but my darkest days were still to come. I didn't just steal from my family, I stole anything I could get my hands on, whether it be truckloads of lumber or goods and equipment straight off other people's property. I could be a complete gentleman when I was sober, but that almost never happened anymore and I was completely ruled by my uncaring attitude about the world and the people around me. The only person I was interested in was me, and I disgusted myself. My body had taken so much abuse that I was shaking all over and hearing voices constantly. I contemplated suicide more times than I could count. I never acted on it, but it was a possibility that I considered just about every day. Probably the only thing that kept me from doing it was the knowledge that the only reality waiting for me after death was hell, and that wouldn't provide any relief from the pain I was already feeling.

My dad was back to drinking heavily, too. One day, after most of the kids had left and he had sold off everything of value on the farm, I was over at the house. My aunt and uncle were visiting from their farm in Dunnville, and they had brought up crates of cucumbers and other food for my parents. As was the custom, they had even brought up some wine for the occasion. Little did they know how disastrous the afternoon was going to turn.

I don't remember what in particular set me off that day, but my anger got the best of me and I got into a fight with my dad. Once he'd had enough of me, he kicked me out of the house and chased me onto the porch with a double-barreled shotgun. He told me that he owned the house and that he wasn't going to put up with me anymore. As I stumbled outside, he told me not to come back, and I was of a mind to accommodate him. I only made it about halfway down the laneway when he pulled the trigger and shot up a field of pellets all around me, hitting me in the back of the leg.

"Pull the trigger," I pleaded. "Do it now. Shoot me."

Limping, I turned around and faced him defiantly. We both knew he had one more bullet in the gun. I was as angry as I had ever been as I put one foot in front of the other and walked right back up to the porch, just a few feet away from where he was standing with the shotgun pointed at me. I grabbed the barrel of the gun and slammed its end against my chest. "Pull the trigger," I pleaded. "Do it now. Shoot me, or I'll put this gun around your neck." I stared into his cold eyes and half-expected to die, but as the seconds ticked by, I could see him soften. He didn't have the guts to kill his own son. Every fiber of my being wanted him to do it, to end my suffering, but he lowered his hand and let me stumble away.

After many traumatic events like this, I couldn't go back and face Sonya, so I took the few possessions I had left and headed west.

My destination was Vancouver, British Columbia. Over the years, some of my brothers and sisters, including my younger sister Claire, had moved to Vancouver to start over. Unfortunately, starting over wasn't in the cards for me and life there turned out to be more of the same, a revolving door of prison cells and months spent passed out on skid row. Drinking and violence were the only two things I knew how to do. I didn't even have an idea of what recovery would involve. I didn't want to try.

Nearly a year went by for me without seeing my wife and kids. At some point during that year, I was hand-delivered an envelope with divorce papers inside. Sonya had finally decided to end her misery.

Most of my days were spent hanging out in Pigeon Park in the worst part of downtown Vancouver. By the close of 1980, I had been drunk for over a year. There was a group of guys like me who lived in the park, all of whom were collecting welfare to get by. Whenever one guy would get his cheque, we drank until it was gone.

By then, another would have gotten a cheque and the whole process would start over again.

Waking up early one morning, I looked around at the guys I was hanging with. They were still passing around a wine bottle as the sun peaked up over the horizon. I was profusely hung-over and could hardly remember who I was, never mind how I had gotten there. My whole body was shaking, and as I looked around at my surroundings, I knew that I couldn't keep living that way. I didn't want to spend the rest of my life in a place like this. I didn't have the answers, I didn't know how I was going to get better, but as I gave serious thought to the divorce papers I had received, I knew where I had to go.

That same afternoon, I walked into the welfare office and picked up enough money to purchase a ticket home. If I was going to divorce Sonya, I was going to at least do it in person. I owed her that much.

> *I looked around at my surroundings, I knew that I couldn't keep living that way. I didn't want to spend the rest of my life in a place like this.*

When I got back to New Credit, Sonya was gracious enough to let me stay with her. She certainly didn't have to, but the alternative would have been staying with my parents, and perhaps she suspected I might not have survived such an arrangement.

A lot had changed since the last time I had seen my family. Sonya and the kids had all given their lives to Jesus at a church on the reserve called New Credit Christian Center. A speaker from out of town had led her to the Lord a couple of years before, about the time I had left to go to the west coast. She and the kids had been praying for me regularly while I was gone, praying that I would find the strength to end my drinking. As it happened, I was still drinking, but since the only reason for my return was to grant Sonya a divorce, I didn't see the point in even trying.

Of course, while I was staying with them, I still wanted to get on Sonya's good side, and the only way to do that was to go to church with them. It was January 7, 1981, just a few weeks after Christmas, and I had no inkling of what was going to happen or how it would forever change the course of my life. I could never have prepared myself for finding Jesus that night, since everything I knew about religion had contributed to the terror and confusion that had been an everyday part of the home I was raised in. The one thing I had known through all my struggles was that if Jesus had been represented by my father and the church we had gone to as children, then I didn't want anything to do with him.

Everything I knew about religion had contributed to the terror and confusion that had been an everyday part of the home I was raised in.

But on this night, I was presented with a drastically different view of faith and the hope it could bring to my life. Instead of merely satisfying my soon to be ex-wife, Jesus came into my life and delivered me from my own self-destruction. I cried for what seemed like hours. As I sat in that small church, I knew for the first time in my life that God was real, and that he had a vested interest in what I did with myself. Not only did I know he was real, but I had a picture of the overflowing love that he had for me. Something happened inside me as I silently poured out my heart to God.

It was as radical and unexpected a turning point as I could have experienced. That night, I proved that even in your darkest moment God is extending a hand to you and patiently waiting for you to accept the full portion of mercy, grace, and forgiveness that has been set aside for you. Life was never the same again.

CHAPTER TWO

The Hand of Violation

CLAIRE 1963-1984

The Sault family could be split into two halves, the oldest eight children and the youngest eight. I was born eight years after Larry, so I definitely fit into the latter category. In some ways, our growing up years were much different. For instance, while our parents had directly raised the first batch of kids, the older kids – particularly the older sisters – had a large hand in taking care of us, the younger half. That being the case, though, our lives weren't really any less violent than those who came before us. Our dad was as unpredictable and terrorizing as ever.

Life was overshadowed from the very beginning by the pressing responsibility of taking care of the farm. As the older kids came and went, we inherited the tasks of cooking, cutting wood, and making sure the harvests were looked after. The pressure was on the younger generation since, with fewer kids around, there was just as much work and fewer slaves to accomplish it.

Our parents supervised a lot of this activity, but our oldest sisters took on the role of surrogate moms. It's a good thing that we had them, because by the third grade our mom began to take prescription drugs. I remember coming home from school and finding her in a heavy sleep. Even though I didn't know exactly what was going on, I knew she wasn't just taking a nap. When she came to, she usually wasn't entirely with it. This became just one more family dysfunction to mix in with the larger picture.

Our family's supposed Christianity was a deeply confusing issue for me.

Religion was a constant presence in my life from the time I was born. While our dad didn't find religion until a year or two after Larry came into the world, I had started out Pentecostal from the word go. Our family's supposed Christianity was a deeply confusing issue for me since at school I was surrounded by teaching related to the Iroquois culture and secular traditions of the Indian people. I call them secular, but my dad would have referred to that as paganism. As part of our school curriculum, we learned how to sing in my mother's native language (Cayuga, spoken by some of the northern Iroquoian tribes), make moccasins, and learn various other traditional items. Most importantly, we learned about the true history of our local Indian people. I had a difficult time reconciling this world with the one my parents raised me in. My dad was adamant that we have nothing to do with traditional Indian life, and even to stay away from kids that came from families that practiced it.

When I was just three years old, I had the first inclinations that there was something wrong with my dad. Erratic behavior and domestic abuse aside, there was something wrong with him – sexually. At first, it was just an intuition, and it forms some of my earliest memories as a child.

My dad was adamant that we have nothing to do with traditional Indian life, and even to stay away from kids that came from families that practiced it.

There were a number of things that happened over the years, but there was one event in particular that proved to be excruciatingly significant. It happened around the time that I was 10. I was in Grade 5 that year, and though I didn't know it at the time, I was going to fail and have to take Grade 5 over again. Now, every once in a while, my dad would arbitrarily keep me home from school for wetting my bed at night, or under the guise of getting some help on a project on the farm. Since education still wasn't a priority, these excuses were never questioned, least of all by my mom. We told her what was going on and, for whatever reason, she chose to do nothing about it. Perhaps she didn't quite know what to do.

On this day, my dad singled me out and told me I wouldn't be going to school with the other kids. After my brothers and sisters had gone off to school, he forced me into their bedroom and raped me. It seemed to go on for hours. I knew without a doubt that what my father was doing to me was so wrong.

While we were in the bedroom, there was a knock at the door, and my dad told me to get up and answer it. It was my older brother Garry waiting at the front door. He had moved out some time previous to this and occasionally came home to visit. My dad quickly made me get dressed, dry off my tears, and answer the door as though nothing was wrong. I was so afraid of what he would do to me if I didn't obey, so I did exactly as he said, stopped crying, and went to meet Garry at the door.

After my brothers and sisters had gone off to school, he forced me into their bedroom and raped me. I knew without a doubt that what my father was doing to me was so wrong.

As soon as he saw my face, he knew something was wrong. For that matter, he had a pretty good idea what it was. "Is what I think happening actually happening?" he whispered softly. He was trying to be as discreet as possible because he was just as afraid of our dad as I was. Standing in front of my brother, I couldn't hold it in. I tried as best I could not to cry, but as I answered him, I began sobbing silently. I gasped over and over, trying to catch my breath, sucking back each tear as it pooled in the bottom of my eye, but I couldn't hold them all in.

The memories of that day continue to hold a great deal of pain for me. The hardest part is remembering the emotions I felt when Garry asked me about what was going on. This event just about destroyed my soul that day. I knew absolutely, positively, and completely that there was no God, that there was no way God could exist and allow that kind of trauma to happen to me. I know that day profoundly impacted my brother as well.

I knew… there was no God, that there was no way God could exist and allow that kind of trauma to happen to me.

Garry tried to stay as long as he could, because he knew the moment he left my dad would pick up where he'd left off. He was trying to protect me as best he could. My dad never came downstairs. Instead he was still in the bedroom, waiting for me to get rid of Garry. I was kind of nervous and worried that my dad would come out and turn on him, and yet I didn't want my brother to leave me with this monster. Thankfully, Garry was stalling and trying to stay with me until it was closer to the time that the school bus would bring the other kids home.

Garry and I have talked about those events later when we were both struggling with alcoholism and trying to find healing. It breaks my heart that he still blamed himself for not doing more. I reminded him that he was just as much a child as I was, and he wasn't a fighter – not like Larry was. I don't doubt that if it had been Larry on the doorstep that day, events would have gone differently. My dad might not have left the house alive. But instead, Garry left, and my dad continued and threatened me by saying that if I told, I would be sent to a training school. Prior to this incident, he would grab at me and touch me every chance he got, even when my mother was home.

That day, when I was sexually violated by my dad, my heart became hardened. That incident shaped my belief systems for the next eighteen years of my life. He started to touch me more and more often as time went on.

I remember sitting in church one morning with my sister. We went to church three or four times a week, about every other day, so our exposure to religious fanaticism was high, but on this occasion I turned to her and asked, "Do you think this is real? Do you think Jesus is real?" The question was legitimate! We were all living such a lie, putting on our smiling faces and showing up in front of our friends in our best clothes, all the while hiding the hurt of what was going on behind closed doors. And yet my sister, who was ten months older than me and had been molested just as much as I had, turned to look at me with wide, appalling eyes. She couldn't even belief that I would question the existence of God in that situation. "Of course he is!" she said back without thinking, making me feel like a fool for even raising the question.

We were always fighting sleep, trying to stay at least half-awake just in case our dad came in to feel us up.

It wasn't uncommon for us to wake up in the middle of the night and have our dad next to us, feeling us. This was something that was consistent even with some of the boys. Later in life, some of my siblings admitted that they had been molested by both my dad and my grandpa. The effect this had on all of us was that we couldn't sleep through the night. We were always fighting sleep, trying to stay at least half-awake just in case our dad came in to feel us up. It wasn't like we all had private rooms, so there were times when my brothers would wake up while he was sexually feeling us, and they didn't know what to do. Some of them later conveyed that they knew what he was doing, but felt powerless to do anything about themselves since they were just children, too. Because of these kinds of experiences, I've never been a good sleeper. To this day, I'm an early riser. I recently began to ask God for restoration and healing for the trauma.

I hated the way my dad used religion to justify the things he was doing to us. When I complained and cried and asked him to stop, he would turn the Bible against us. "Abraham slept with his daughters," he would righteously argue. "If it was acceptable in the Old Testament, then it's acceptable now." But that wasn't his only excuse. Sometimes he would talk about his buddies, using them as examples for his own parental ideals. "So-and-so sexually molests his daughters, and they never complain about it. They even enjoy it! Why can't you?"

One of the most difficult truths to grapple with is the degree to which my mom let these terrible things happen to us. She didn't so much as lift a finger in our defense. Instead, she would load my brothers in the car and leave my sisters and I alone with him on repeated occasions. She would say bizarre things, like "Was your dad bothering you today?" She would even sound concerned about it. To this, I would answer, "Yes." And I could barely get the words out, because I had absolutely no respect for her and her inability to protect us or take charge, as a mother should. *Bothering us.* That's what she referred to his sexual abuse as. Even though she did, at times, seem concerned, it was never enough for her to take any protective action. Perhaps she feared him as much as I did.

My sisters saw straight through my dad's excuses as well. If my dad held me back in the morning and said we were going to be spending the day working on the tractor, my sister knew exactly what was in store for me. I would beg her not to go to school, to stay home with me. "Oh no," she would say. "I know what's going to happen to me if I do." I'm sure my plight would be on her mind all day at school. When she got home later, I would rage out and take my anger out on her for abandoning me and leaving me with that monster.

Despite my anger, she was the only person that I felt close to at that time. My anger toward her was completely misdirected. Thankfully, years later we were able to talk about these things and share the anger and sorrow that we both felt.

Later that year, two of my older sisters decided to rescue us from the situation. While we were at school one day, they showed up and took us out of class. They told us that we were running away from home and heading out west. I can hardly describe just how happy I was! I thought we were really going to get out of the violent, sexual mess we were in. It was early in the afternoon when they came to get us, close to 2:00 pm, and they took us into nearby Brantford to hide out.

My parents must have realized that we weren't coming back after a few hours passed and none of us had showed up at home, so they called the police. To this day, I still haven't figured out how they knew where we were, but at 2:00 in the morning the next day, a police cruiser pulled up to where we were hiding out and escorted us back home. When all four of us had been collected, the police asked us why we had run away, and my older sisters told them exactly what kind of abuse was going on under our parents' roof.

Unfortunately, there probably wasn't very much that the police could do to help us. In the early 1970s, the government's policy toward the Indian reservations was convoluted and laced with controversy. Because of the political autonomy granted to the Indian nations, the police had their hands tied when getting mixed up with our business. They couldn't really get too involved since our reservation was off-limits. So regardless of our story, and whether they believed it or not, they brought us home. My sisters' hearts were in the right place, but in the end all they achieved was a 12-hour vacation from our father's cruelty.

When I was 12, there an incident in which my parents were arguing throughout the day about whether I would help with the dishes or help dad with a project out in the yard. By this time, I was pretty adept at picking up on my dad's code, so I knew that what I'd really be doing was spending the day being sexually abused by him. When it came time to go outside, I went along with it out of fear of my dad. Just as I was walking outside, though, I heard the door open behind me. When I looked back, my mom was marching toward me, obviously mad. When she got to me, she punched me right in the face. The blood started to flow. This was the first time my nose had bled, and I remember watching my mom go back into the house, realizing just how bad this no-win situation I was in was. As young as I was, I knew she was angry with him and was misdirecting it at me, when she should have been punching *him* in the nose.

I guess it's not surprising that I began lashing out at school. Just like Larry before me, I got into a lot of fights and became a bully. I wasn't afraid of anybody. I didn't hesitate to fight with guys that were twice my size. When I looked into the CAS (Children's Aid Society) records later in life, I found out that my odd behavior had been reported to social services. I was happy to see this in writing, because for years I had felt angry under the assumption that no one, including the professionals, recognized what was going on or did anything about it. When I saw how many times these events were reported, I melted in forgiveness toward them.

It must have been pretty obvious to outsiders what was going on, a fact that was confirmed by the kinds of questions my sister and I started getting from the public health nurse at the school. She sat us both down in the nurse's room, separately, and asked, "Are you being touched in your private area?" There it was, right out in the open, an opportunity to speak the truth. My sister was scared, so she said, "No." I wasn't about to let this chance slip by me, and so I looked the nurse right in the eyes and told the truth. "Yes! I am!" So the teachers knew, because they were the ones reporting to the public health nurse.

Despite finally being able to verbalize the reality of the situation, though, nothing happened. There was no hero coming to our rescue, least of all the government bodies who were supposed to be looking out for us. According to the documentation, when our mother was questioned about the situation, her answer seemed to satisfy them. She said that she had asked our dad and that he had denied it. She assured the social workers that she would protect us. But she didn't.

My anger escalated the older I got and the longer the situation went unresolved, and the most obvious target for this anger became my mother. At one point when I was in Grade 8, my dad moved to Cleveland to work for a period of time. My parents were having marital problems. Although it was a relief to be free of my dad's violent and sexual hand, spending so much extra time with my mom did nothing to relieve the rage I was feeling.

I felt like Cinderella living under her evil stepmother.

She was an impatient woman, to say the least. I could never move fast enough for her or get enough done. First, all of us girls would do the dishes, sweep the floor, and iron baskets of laundry ... I felt like Cinderella living under her evil stepmother. Nothing was ever good enough for her. It didn't matter how much or how quickly we did the chores, she never told us what a good job we had done.

One afternoon, in a rebellious moment, I was taking my time sweeping the floor when she came careening into the room, grabbed the broom from my hand, and smacked me in the head with it. I turned to her, seething. "You do that again and I'll hit you back. I mean business." I was purposefully trying to provoke her, hoping she would explode back. I desperately wanted an excuse to harm her and let loose all the anger and disrespect I had for her. As she stood, waiting for me to pick up the broom and continue working, I smiled inside and flopped down on the couch. I pulled out a photo album and browsed through some of the pictures, waiting to see what she'd do next.

It worked perfectly. She jerked the photo album out of my hand and hit me over the head with it. I didn't waste a second. I stood up and jerked the album right back from her, sitting back down with it. I wanted to convey the message that I no longer feared her.

Maybe it had worked a little too perfectly. That same day, she phoned up the Children's Aid office of southern Ontario and told the social workers that she had lost control of me. She told them that I was raging for no reason at all and that she was scared I was going to hurt her. Well, at least she got one part right. Given another chance, I would have done just that. According to my mother, though, my behavior was entirely unprovoked, and there was something mentally wrong with me. This is what the documents inferred.

Children's Aid came within a few days and removed me from the home. I tried telling the social workers what was really going on, but they seemed happy to take my mom's word over mine. "She's a nutcase!" I argued. "She drags me around by the hair! She kicks me around the living room like a football when she's angry!" But my words fell on deaf ears. They put me in foster care with a couple elsewhere on the reserve.

I tried telling the social workers what was really going on, but they seemed happy to take my mom's word over mine.

Four months later, I temporarily went to a group home. It was after that ordeal that the social workers told me I had two choices of where to go next to live. The first option was a Christian family on the reserve. The moment they said that word "Christian," my stomach turned. After the experiences I'd had with my parents and church, there was no way I was going to live with Christians. I was 13 and knew one thing above all others: there was no such thing as God. When I asked about the other option, I was told, "Well, you could go home and give your mom another chance." My face said it all, I'm sure. There was no way I was going to put myself through that again, especially knowing that my dad had moved back to the reserve from Cleveland and that my mom hadn't told the social workers that small detail. Small, indeed!

It was the fall of 1977, and faced with the prospect of not having a home to go to, I decided to start making my own decisions. I would be better off left to my own devices than to settle with either of those options. First, however, I called my sister, who was living in Vancouver at the time. When I told her what was happening, she was really concerned and immediately suggested that I move west and live with her. She was a big proponent of getting yourself to safety.

She was finally finding some stability in her life there and wanted to help me out in any way she could.

But I wasn't ready to move all the way across the country just yet. Instead, I went job hunting in Brantford. My plan was to find steady work and support myself. Of course, nobody would hire a 13-year-old girl, so I had to lie about my age. It didn't take long to find employment at a local factory that manufactured electric curling irons. They paid me $2.80 an hour. Considering the cost of living and the economic environment, that was a decent wage. I called my sister, who was still living at home, and told her about the job at the factory and that she could work there, too. I suggested that we lie about our age and she could leave my parents home and move in with me in Brantford. She didn't need much convincing, and before long we were living together in a small apartment, paying $160 per month in rent. That included utilities.

We tried that for six months, but we began to party more than we worked. Needless to say, we lost our jobs and abandoned our apartment because of our obvious instability. This time I was ready for a more drastic change, and so I packed my bags and headed for the Greyhound station. I was finally taking my sister up on her offer.

My sights were set on Vancouver.

The first thing I did in Vancouver was get a job – at McDonald's. The service industry came naturally to me. As a hostess, my job was to go around to all the customers and serve coffee and pretty much just be pleasant to them. I was good at it. Really good.

When we were kids, our dad used to host mid-week Bible studies or some sort of church event at our house for the church we went to. As soon as people started to arrive, we had to act like the hosts, taking their jackets and serving the food and drinks. We were glorified caterers. What was so ironic about these meetings is that we may have just been on the receiving end of a beating, being kicked around the floor or worse, but as soon as the knock on the door came, we had to wipe away the tears and be on our best behavior. As sick as that was, I discovered my natural skills as a hostess this way. It was my first insight into an important skill set that would eventually come to serve me well in life.

My first glimpses of self-worth also coincided with my discovery of alcohol.

I started off working the early morning shift, which meant that I was serving the older crowd. The customers took a liking to me, complimenting me and wanting to know why I was working at McDonald's. "What are you doing working here? You're far too smart for this place." As usual, the main reason was that I didn't have any work experience. After all, I was a 14-year-old pretending to be older in order to support myself. This was probably the first time in my life that I started to believe that I had something going for me, and it made me feel good about myself.

Unfortunately, my first glimpses of self-worth also coincided with my discovery of alcohol. I have an obsessive personality by nature, so as soon as I started drinking, I was doing so excessively. My alcoholism escalated faster than I could ever have anticipated. I was living with the crippling pain of what my parents had done to me, and the only time I could escape it was when I popped open a bottle. It was like a medicine that soothed my soul and allowed me a short reprieve from how I really felt about myself inside. From day one,

I was experiencing blackouts and binging my way through entire weekends, putting myself in some pretty dangerous situations. There were times when I woke up in lockup with no memory of having gotten there. I would be in the drunk tank, surrounded by skid row prostitutes, and I was too afraid to ask someone if they knew what had happened to get me there.

Through all this, I managed to maintain my day job, and considering how disconcerting the blackouts were, that was quite an accomplishment. I didn't see this lifestyle as being abnormal, since I had been surrounded with it since I was a kid. My dad had lived that way, as had all of my brothers and sisters. I was a product of the environment I had come from, and didn't know any other way to live.

Knowing there wasn't a heaven or a hell to go to made suicide seem like the most obvious escape from the nightmare that was my life.

With the onset of my heavy drinking came a new crowd of street-type friends that were as bad for me as the poison I was consuming by the bottle. Over the course of the next few years, circumstances continued to decline. A few months after I turned 15, I was no longer living with sister, but rather at a boyfriend's house.

One weekend in the middle of one of my binges, I made the knee-jerk decision to commit suicide. Knowing there wasn't a heaven or a hell to go to made suicide seem like the most obvious escape from the nightmare that was my life, so I went into the bathroom cabinet and found a bottle of pills my friend's mother was taking for her heart. In the throes of depression, I took as many of them as I could get in my mouth and collapsed out on the bathroom floor to die.

When I woke up, I found myself lying in a bed at Vancouver General Hospital, disoriented and confused. The doctor looking after me told me that I was going to be all right and then recommended that I book an appointment with a psychiatrist. Out of curiosity, I followed up on the referral and decided to see what this shrink would have to say about me.

This meeting represented the first time that I realized there were more messed-up people in the world than me. It came as a shock, but when you're as self-absorbed and living in your own head as I was, you assume that you're the only one who suffers from the kind of deep problems I had on my mind. I don't know what I expected to come of my meeting with the psychiatrist, but surely it wasn't anything like what I got. The woman sat me down and ranted for an hour about how rotten men were, and how they were all the same and wouldn't get any better. From the psychiatrist! I sat there on the chair silently and listened to this vile. I had enough sense at least to realize that this woman probably needed as much help as I did, because she looked to be about 50 whereas I was still a teenager. Being young seemed to at least give me an excuse for not having it all together.

I tried getting my lifestyle under control, but my success was decidedly mixed. Using nothing but willpower, I would sometimes stop drinking for a month at a time, but something would always happen that made me feel like I had no choice but to start again. I couldn't seem to get my life back on track.

During one of my sober periods, my brother was in town and came to see me. Even though he was still drinking, he was tender-hearted toward the Lord and continued to have faith in His power to restore. He tried to share the Gospel with me, but I didn't want to have anything to do with it. "Don't talk to me about your Jesus," I told him. "I don't want to know." I was full of bitterness and continued living in chaos despite the best efforts of those around me.

My denial was really strong, though I still had a long way to go before hitting rock bottom. I could still look at other people in my family and see that they were much worse off than I was. Larry, for instance, was living through the worst of his addiction in Pigeon Park. In addition to the drinking, he was sniffing glue and downing shaving lotion, anything to get a high. The bus I took to get to work went past the park, through skid row, and sometimes I would look out the bus window and see him lying on the street. It broke my heart to see my brother like that, just another bum, another Indian statistic on skid row. As bad as I felt for him, though, it was easy to forget how quickly I was slipping into the same trap. I was just barely surviving myself! I'd like to say that seeing Larry at his worst helped wake me up, but it didn't.

By the time I was 17, I was still trying to balance my out of control drinking with my efforts to get my high school equivalency from Vancouver Community College. I was still working a full-time job and losing my weekends to alcohol. Monday mornings were the worst, with me making my way to work sicker than a dog, completely hung-over, with the smell of booze on my breath.

A couple of my sisters became extremely concerned about the kind of life I was living and tried to intervene. They were both sober by this time, having gone through a lot of the same experiences I was having on a regular basis. They had come in contact with Alcoholics Anonymous and had both seen some success through the program. In fact, one of my sisters was about to receive her one-year cake, a reward for being sober for an entire year. To be honest, I didn't entirely understand what she was talking about, but I agreed to go with her to a meeting to celebrate the occasion because it seemed like the honorable thing to do.

I still didn't see myself as being as bad a drunk as she had been, though. When I remembered some of the states she had gotten herself into, I was able to laugh off my own problems, thinking she had been more messed up than I ever would be. That's how sick I was.

I attended the meeting with her and watched as she got her one-year cake. When it came time for the group to talk, everybody went around the circle and introduced themselves in the typical way, saying "My name is so-and-so, and I'm an alcoholic." When it got to me, though, I changed it up a little bit. "My name is Claire," I began, "and I'm a friend of AA." As soon as I closed my mouth, people in the group started laughing. I wondered what was funny about what I'd said, but I soon realized they were laughing at me. For an entire year, my sister had been telling them about me and how badly I needed help. The truth is that the group had me at a disadvantage, since there were very few details of my drinking that they didn't already know. The thing I didn't understand was how ridiculous it was for me to walk in and claim not to be an alcoholic myself … I wasn't fooling anybody. They had the inside scoop, and in a lot of ways understood me better than I understood myself.

Still, I didn't go back for a while. My sisters were pouring it on strong with the AA propaganda – at least that's how I viewed it – but I wasn't open to what they were saying. The thing I was most resistant to was the concept of accepting the authority of a higher power in my life. I still thought I could exercise enough control over my habit to get by in the real world. Whether it was God they were talking about, or Jesus in particular, I simply didn't want a part of that. "You just go ahead and keep your Jesus to yourself, because that works for you. Trust me, it doesn't work for me."

I wasn't interested, and I stayed that way for another year. At 18, I finally started to seriously recognize that I needed to do something to drastically change the direction I was heading in. In addition to my drinking habit, my drug abuse was spiraling out of control, getting worse by the day.

One of the few things I did recreationally besides alcohol and drugs was play on a women's fastball team. Through my involvement in the sport, I came into contact with an older Metis woman who took an interest in me. She came up to me one day after a game and befriended me, encouraging me that I had great leadership abilities on the team. To be honest, I didn't really see it. I didn't believe her, but it was a nice thing to hear. It was actually a strange bit of interaction since I didn't know her from Adam. Anyway, even though she was a complete stranger, she kept talking to me and telling me about how good I was at the sport. No one had told me that before, and it was uncomfortable for me to accept praise. I didn't think much of it in the beginning, but looking back now I'm pretty confident it was a divine appointment, that the Lord was orchestrating the meeting behind the scenes.

Her encouragement became a welcome part of my week, but it wasn't in and of itself enough to pull me out of my downward spiral. By the time I turned 20, I was hanging out with the guys on skid row. I didn't know it, but it's likely I was drinking in the same circles Larry had come and gone from just a few years before me. I was starting to lose my last grip on normal life, sliding further and further away from the front I tried to put up during the week.

The timing was too perfect for God not to have had a hand in it.

Since my first suicide attempt, I had continued to contemplate ending my own life and made a couple more attempts. On one particular day in August of 1984, I once again hit that low. I was hung-over after being drunk for ten days and felt just terrible about myself. I don't know how, but my sister somehow knew the dire straits I was in, because she called the Metis woman and told her what was going on. Her and her husband showed up at my door unannounced that day, probably not knowing that I had been planning my suicide all day. If they hadn't showed up at the exact time they did, I'm certain that I wouldn't be here today to tell the story. Once again, the timing was too perfect for God not to have had a hand in it. This couple would later have a profound impact on introducing me to a Jesus that loved me just the way I was.

That's the day that I found out that the Metis woman was not only a Christian, but also an Alanon member. Thankfully, she hadn't ever told me about the Christian part, or I would have ran from her as fast as I could. Her husband told me about how he had been sober for a number of years and attributed his success to the AA program. I was at my lowest point as they were telling me this, and so I made the decision to give AA a chance. From that point on, I became committed to sobering up and going through the program.

Together, my sister and my friend helped get me into a treatment program in northern British Columbia, where I was about to undergo one of the most intense experiences of my life: cold-turkey detox.

CHAPTER THREE

Freedom Through Grace

LARRY 1981-1993

As profound an experience as it was for me when I got saved, my adjustment back to the real world was just as important. Sonya and I called off the divorce, and I moved back in with my family full-time. I was determined to provide for them, so one of the first things I did was go back to the Ironworkers.

It was a difficult transition for me to make since the guys there were pretty rough. The language on the job was terrible now that I was more aware of how it affected me. A lot of the guys brought pornography with them to work and looked at it every chance they got. In that way, it was probably a pretty ordinary construction site, but I had changed and had to now find a way to work in it and maintain the new lifestyle I had adopted. It wasn't easy, since they were constantly trying to pull me back into their circles.

I didn't hide from them the fact that I had become a Christian, but I didn't flaunt it, either. It wasn't my style just to walk up to these guys and start preaching at them, but I would often have pamphlets and books with me that I was reading during my lunch breaks. Even the Bible. So while they were looking at porn magazines, I was reading the Bible. You can imagine what was being said behind my back! I'm sure they were talking about me a lot, and we would all laugh it off and make jokes.

I didn't hide from them the fact that I had become a Christian, but I didn't flaunt it, either.

The only thing I knew to do to keep from succumbing to the same destructive habits of the past was to separate myself from the other guys. The more I tried to stay away, the harder they tried to break me down. Before I'd gotten saved, when I worked as an Ironworker, I was always the guy with the money, buying drinks for the others. Now the tables had been turned on me. Suddenly, the guys would pull up to my house with several cases of beer and try to convince me to get in with them. Sometimes it took a lot to say no to them, but I stayed consistent for the first year, keeping my distance from anything that could get me into trouble. Eventually, they started to leave me alone. I never got violent with any of them or raised my voice, but as I got more comfortable witnessing to them about my own experiences, they finally got the message and started dropping away from me like flies.

It was clear to me that I needed new friends, which led me and my family to getting more involved in the local church. In the early 1980s, the Word of Faith movement was beginning to infiltrate the reservation, and a number of pastors in the area were getting together to organize a new Bible school. It was called the Liberty Bible Training Center, and it seemed to be the answer to my prayers. In the fall of 1981, my wife and I enrolled in the school and were accepted into the charter class. It was the perfect opportunity to start making new associations.

> ## It was clear to me that I needed new friends, which led me and my family to getting more involved in the local church.

I hadn't joined the school because I wanted to be a preacher. In fact, I didn't want anything to do with ministry. All of the junk we had learned growing up in Pentecostal churches had made sure of that, even though the Word of Faith message was a lot different than all the things I'd heard before. What I wanted out of Bible school was as much information as possible. I wanted to know everything I could about God and what the Bible had to say.

My favorite verse came from 2 Corinthians 5:17. *Therefore if any man be in Christ, he is a new creature: old things are passed away; behold, all things are become new* (KJV). The words of the apostle Paul came alive in me, and so I used to quote that all the time. As a new Christian, it was something I could think about that brought back all the emotions I had when I first got saved. It got me so excited!

In the fall, Sonya and I decided to move the family off the reservation and go to Mississauga, Ontario to be closer to the school. It was a big step since it was the first time we moved as a family away from New Credit. We both had to get full-time jobs to support the family, so I found work as the manager of a nearby gas bar and she supervised at a women's clothing store. Even when it was tough to make ends meet, God was faithful to help us. I bought a lot of tapes and invested a lot of money in ministry tools in order to make sure I had the best information possible about God's Word. I was so eager and excited to learn about this new life that I was walking through.

When Claire stopped drinking, she had the support system of AA to help her stay on track, but for me all I had was the Bible. I wanted to do anything and everything it said. Fortunately, that was enough. As of January 7, 1981, I managed to give up cigarettes and alcohol all at once. Only by the grace of God!

When Claire stopped drinking, she had the support system of AA to help her stay on track, but for me all I had was the Bible. Fortunately, that was enough.

My wife and I started leading the children's ministry at the church we were attending and we ended up growing it to about 60 kids. From there, we moved up to youth ministry. I was also doing a lot of the grounds keeping, so I think it's fair to say I was involved in a lot of different areas. Maybe I was involved in too much.

One Sunday, I was sitting in one of the front rows listening to the pastor encouraging the people to do more for the church. After having been on my best behavior for so many months, I finally lost my temper. The longer I sat, the angrier I got. All I could think about was the number of times I had sweated all day out in the sun, cutting the grass at the new church offices that had just been renovated while the pastor sat in his air-conditioned office with his books, studying. As church let out, I was so mad I could hardly speak. I ran out, jumped in my car, and went home. Sonya knew I was angry, but she didn't know why. I didn't say a word to her before leaving her behind with the kids and driving to Buffalo, New York.

I went straight to the first bar I could find and started drinking. I got drunk, *drunk* drunk, and I stayed that way for six months. By this time, I had finished my year at Bible school, and had all the time in the world to go back to the same old lifestyle. Every once in a while, I would show up at church and couldn't wait to stand outside the front door and light up a cigarette. I wanted everyone to see what had happened to me. I wanted to hurt them. Especially the pastor. I wanted to blow smoke in his face and somehow get even for what I had been put through.

It took six months for me to realize what an idiot I was and that the only person I was hurting was myself. When I'd gotten saved, I had given up my addictions, the drugs and the cigarettes and the alcohol, but the one thing I hadn't been able to get rid of was the anger still seething inside. As soon as I came out of my half-year binge, I bought a stack of books on anger management so that I could take steps to make sure I wouldn't over-react every time somebody did or said something to me I didn't like.

I found out that Kenneth Copeland, one of my favorite ministers, was going to be speaking in Detroit. I was able to identify with him more than some of the other preachers in the Word of Faith circles, probably because of his background; he came from a life that I understood. Backslidden as I was, I made my way to Detroit and stood in the back of the convention hall and found my way back to the Lord. With Sonya at my side, I recommitted my life and never looked back.

The hardest thing I had to do upon returning to the church was make amends to the pastor I had violated. Nobody had told me to do this, but God was speaking to my heart. *I want you to go apologize*, he said. *Apologize first to the pastor, then ask to stand before the congregation and apologize to them, too.* I can hardly put into words just how hard this was for me. I would have rather punched my pastor than apologize to him. My anger toward him had been building for so long. I resented him for taking it literally that a man of God should study to the exclusion of all else while people like me took care of all the dirty work and heavy lifting. I didn't want to be humble; I wanted to attack him! That's certainly what my dad would have done! And it was my first instinct, too, but God was softening me up and showing me that there was a better way. Once I apologized to everyone involved, I felt an incredible emotional release unlike anything I'd experienced before. At last, I was free from the anger that had consumed me.

I started ministering to the church and God was honoring everything I put my hand to.

Sonya and I continued in that ministry for another three years. In addition to what I had been doing before my breakdown, I was now involved in music ministry. Most importantly, I was even doing some speaking. I started ministering to the church and God was honoring everything I put my hand to.

By the end of the three years, people in the church were calling Sonya and I for counseling. From what I understood about authority, though, this wasn't my area and I didn't want to have anything to do with it. The last thing I wanted to do was violate the leadership that was already in place. In my view, the problem was that the pastor was not really a people person and he wasn't very good at dealing with real issues. I was nervous with treading onto dangerous ground, so I just told people that I wasn't the pastor. As excited and enthusiastic as I was about ministry, I wasn't going to go there.

Unfortunately, the counseling and speaking requests kept coming in, and the pastor seemed to get insecure about our position in the church. At least, that's the way I saw it. Since I was already stepping out of our home church and helping out other Native pastors with fledgling ministries, it occurred to me that perhaps it was time to move on. I had already been ordained by that time, and so together with Sonya we decided that it was time to leave the church.

I scheduled a meeting with our pastor and talked to him about what was on my mind and my perception that he thought I was overstepping my authority in the church. My motives were pure in having the discussion, because I wanted everything to be out in the open. I was completely surprised when he turned things around on me, accusing me of trying to split the church! "It seems like every time a good church gets going, the devil rises up and causes a split." I couldn't believe it! From his point of view, I was no better than the devil. Splitting the church had never so much as crossed my mind, and I told him so.

In the end, I kept my cool as best I could and casually informed him that Sonya and I had already made the decision to go our separate way. I wish we could have left that church under better circumstances because I had become attached to a lot new friends in that church family. But ultimately, God had bigger and better things in store for me.

The prospect of having the opportunity to minister to so many people really made me excited.

I'm not sure whether I would call it a vision or a dream, but when I was attending Bible school in Mississauga, I had a vivid dream in which I was ministering to the Chinese ... or at least, I thought they were Chinese, and if not that then certainly of Asian descent. There were masses and masses of them, thousands of people, standing as far back as the eye could see. The prospect of having the opportunity to minister to so many people really made me excited, but I didn't have any idea how or when such a thing would come about.

Shortly after setting out on our own, I got an invitation to speak in the Arctic with an Assemblies of God preacher named John Spillenaar. He was an older gentleman who was conducting a conference in the Canadian Arctic, and he wanted to bring me along. I was thrilled to join him, and raised my own money so that I could go without being a financial liability to the meetings. In fact, I paid my own way most of the time in those early days, partly because I didn't know enough to ask. While we were ministering to a huge crowd of Inuit, I felt God speak to my heart again. *Remember those people you saw in the vision? These are them.* I ended up making numerous trips up to the Arctic in the ensuing years.

Simultaneous to my trips into the north, in 1984 I received a call from the chief of my home community at New Credit. The chief knew who I was and also knew my story, having overcome alcoholism to become a traveling minister. It seemed that I was beginning to be an up and coming influential member of the community, which is why the chief and council, the governing body of our reservation, wanted to know if I was interested in sitting on a committee.

The politics of Indian country were fascinating back then, and remain so today, but I'll give you some context for what was taking place in Canada at that time. Up until the late 60s and early 70s, the Canadian government under Prime Minister Pierre Elliot Trudeau was controlling everything that went on in Native reservations. The part of the government that was responsible for this was known as Indian Affairs. Officials would come into our communities on a monthly basis and hold meetings about the future of the Indian territories. The government's policy of assimilation was not working, and so in dealing with the "Indian problem," the Minister of Indian Affairs introduced to us the concept of self-government.

> *The... government thought the Indian people would utterly fail. ...To the surprise of everyone, exactly the opposite happened.*

In the early 70s, the reservations were starting to take on their own responsibilities for administrating the programs and services that directly affected our people. By doing this, the Trudeau government thought the Indian people would utterly fail. According to a widely distributed paper that was released by Indian Affairs, it was projected that the Indians would sink under the weight of their own problems and end up assimilating into the larger population of Canada by 1975. To the surprise of everyone, exactly the opposite happened. As soon as the communities starting taking charge over their own affairs, they began to see great success.

Because there was such widespread alcoholism and drug abuse going on in the First Nations, the Canadian government made it a priority to set up treatment centers that would allow qualified Native professionals to help other Natives in the environment of the reservations. This brings us back to 1984, when the chief and council made their invitation to me. They had seen the extraordinary transformation my life had taken and wanted me to be a part of bringing a treatment center to the Mississaugas of New Credit. The committee I would be a part of would be negotiating with Health Canada to build a 15-bed facility on the reservation.

I didn't have to think twice about the proposal. I accepted the appointment right away. There were so many people in our community who were hurt from precisely these kinds of addictions, including my entire family, and here was a chance to really do something to help. From that day forward, my political involvement in Indian country only grew stronger and more complicated.

Now, I have to say that the church taught me well. Had it not been for the opportunities I had to study the Word of God and speak in the Christian world, both in local churches and on missionary outreaches, I never would have been prepared for the learning curve I was confronted with in the political arena.

When the committee finally got off the ground, it was 1985, and we were negotiating together with fourteen other reservations for the treatment center. After two years of negotiations and proposals, we finally won the bid. Being a part of that process, and seeing it come to fruition, was an incredibly satisfying experience. In fact, it only whetted my appetite for more.

In 1987, I ran for a seat on the First Nation Council. I was still traveling widely throughout the country and preaching while I was in the middle of this campaign, which made for a busy time. Even though I was busy and being pulled in many different directions, I didn't want to sacrifice the ministry aspects of my life. On the community level, I had no strong desire to hold any position of authority – I'm still not motivated by those things– but I pursued politics because I saw an opportunity for me to change the course of our society through policy development. My confidence was bolstered by the success I had seen through my time on the health committee, and I felt like we could parlay that success into broader areas.

One of the greatest joys of that campaign was running alongside my brother Wayne. By the time of the election in late 1987, we had both won seats on the council. Unfortunately, the victory was short-lived. In our naivety, we had no idea what we were getting ourselves into. By the time 1988 came along, we were in the political fight of our lives just to hold on to position we had been elected to.

As a man of integrity, I felt strongly that the political process be conducted openly and honestly.

I was sadly mistaken when I made the assumption that everybody else on council had the same vision I did and wanted to see the same changes happen in the way business was conducted. I felt it was my duty to speak the truth, so I started talking openly to our constituents about what was going on behind the closed doors of council meetings. As a man of integrity, I felt strongly that the political process be conducted openly and honestly.

Needless to say, I ruffled a lot of feathers, the chief's among them. The chief didn't appreciate the fact that he couldn't control or intimidate me. I certainly would not be controlled after living all my growing up years this way.

My brother wasn't quite as aggressive as I was, but I was the rebel on the council and was the one leading the pack. Without including my brother and I in the discussions, the council tried to pass a motion to stop me from publishing public newsletters every month explaining what was really happening at the council level. As far as the chief was concerned, if any information left the council room, it was going to go through him. Regardless of the fact that I didn't see it that way, the entire council proceeded to try and force me out.

What had been intended only for good in my heart ended up bringing about destruction.

I resisted it because the Indian Act was very clear about my authority, having been elected to the council. My seat had been secured democratically, and there was a process in place to have me removed from that seat had I, in fact, been guilty of an offence that dictated my removal. I wasn't guilty of anything like that, so we took our fight to court and fought for eight months on the legality of that action. It was probably one of the worst emotional experiences of my life, aside from the stress I had gone through as a child, and I felt completely drained at the end of it. In court, I was accused of so many things I hadn't had any hand in. Even though I was faced with losing everything I owned, I wouldn't back down from my position. I did what I believed to be right and I stood up for it. What had been intended only for good in my heart ended up bringing about destruction.

The situation got really bad. My kids were in high school at the time, and they would come home from school and say, "Dad, why don't you just leave this thing alone? Why can't you just drop it?" This confirmed to me that the families of the kids my children went to school with were talking about me and what was going on in the courtroom. I sat my kids down and explained my side to them. "You know, in life you're going to be dealt challenges. There's nothing you can do about that. If you believe in your heart that what you're doing is right, you have to stand up and speak the truth."

At the end of eight months, the court ruled in my favor and I was given back my seat. You can imagine the chilly reception I got when I walked back into the council room for the first time. The worst part of the court's decision as far as the chief was concerned was that he had to compensate me in back pay for all the time I had spent away from council. He was so angry with me, he asked me to leave the room when I showed up to my first meeting back. As soon as I had a chance to speak, I apologized for the trouble that had been caused throughout the process. Even though I had been proven right and the court battle hadn't been my fault, I still humbled myself before them. After I said my piece, the chief asked me to excuse myself for a few minutes while the council discussed the situation. I gracefully stepped out of the meeting.

When I was called back in, the chief stood up and said, "We've decided to appeal the court decision." I was completely taken aback, having not realized just how badly they wanted me gone. Some of the other council members could see through the chief's motives and knew what he was really trying to do, which was exercise his own brand of control over the community. In the end, the ruling was upheld, and I received my back pay. It was several years, though, before I returned to the council.

A short time after the chief launched his appeal, he called me into his office for a meeting. I didn't know what to expect, but surely what ended up happening was the farthest thing from anything I could have guessed. He shut the door behind me and said, "Larry, I see some real leadership qualities in you." I was immediately suspicious of where he was going with this, especially since another election was going to be coming up soon. "I hope the fight we're in doesn't put an end to our relationship," he continued. "The truth is, I would like to mentor you."

Before he could get finished, my old anger was already rising up in me. Mentor me? I wanted to put him on the floor, that's what I wanted to do. Fortunately, I resisted my natural urges. "As much as I appreciate the thought, Chief, I think it's pretty obvious that your idea of leadership and mine are miles apart. I'm not interested." With that, I thanked him and walked out.

This was in 1989, and I felt he was trying to exercise some control over me by asking such a question. The meeting had taken the opposite route, however, and I soon announced my intention to run for chief myself. Unfortunately, that campaign wasn't successful and the old guard managed to hold on for another term.

During the summer of 1988, just as my fight with the council was winding down, I started seeking God to prepare my heart for unknown events that I felt were coming down the pipe. For whatever reason, my heart was heavy, and I had an idea that things were going to happen that I wasn't prepared to deal with. "Lord, help me to be stable through whatever life has in store for me, good or bad." I didn't have any particular premonition, but it seemed to me like trouble was brewing on the horizon.

Sure enough, our family was struck by tragedy in October. My brother Wayne, much like my other siblings, had struggled constantly with alcohol, alternating between long binges and periods of being clean and sober in which he regularly attended church and seemed to all eyes to have his life together. Now, I'm not sure what set off that year's bender, but I can say with certainty that the political intrigue didn't help. One night, Wayne got behind the wheel of a car pretty drunk and ended up in a really bad accident. He was killed.

With my presence on the council in limbo, I was back to working steel and iron. Following Wayne's funeral, I was on a construction site that had me up on the steel a few floors off the ground. I was trying to work, but I was tormented by the events surrounding Wayne's death. My whole mind was consumed with heaven and hell, questions of eternity and destiny. In the midst of my anguish, I remember hearing God speak to me, stopping me in the middle of my questions. *Don't go there*, he was saying. *Heaven and hell, these aren't your issues, and they never will be. Leave it alone.*

In the midst of my anguish, I remember hearing God speak to me.

I was cured that day of entertaining those kinds of thoughts. If you're not careful, they will consume you. In fact, I was so far off the ground and not paying attention to what I was doing, I could easily have killed myself worrying about my brother's fate.

In the aftermath of Wayne's passing, I continued ministering. Despite everything, I found myself preoccupied with the notion of returning in some way to the political scene. I was fascinated by the issues and challenges of implementing true self-government on the reservations. Many evenings were spent in my office studying the subject. I even began attending conferences and national think tanks devoted to the discussion of self-governance. It was amazing how much I was able to accomplish and learn as a community member without having any political status at all. By the time the next set of elections came up, in 1993, I knew more about self-government than many of the elected officials in my community.

I didn't miss being in office, though. I missed the influence I had, but politics was something I was almost glad to be rid of. Between traveling and building churches in the Arctic, I still had a lot on my plate

Because of my history with the First Nation Council, I became the go-to person in situations where people on the reservation were opposing the activities of the council. For example, when the community discovered that the chief and council were planning on opening a liquor-licensed establishment on the reserve – the first ever! – a lot of citizens were enraged. I was one of them! The destructive effects of alcohol were profound in my family and in the lives of so many people I knew and grew up with. My own brother had lost his life. Finding out that the chief was working to make alcohol even more freely available came as an absolute shock to me, and I pledged to do anything I could to stop it.

I was selected by a majority of community members to be the spokesperson of the cause, and we hired a lawyer to help us put together a motion to officially designate our community as dry. We weren't going to sit back while the chief held secret meetings about new licensed establishments, so we had our voices heard. Ultimately, we won that case. More than that, it was the beginning of the end for the chief and the kind of politics he stood for.

In 1993, I ran again for chief on a mandate of transparency in government, of taking the open and honest approach in our dealings, of making sure that the community was in the loop on the major issues that affected them. After a fiercely fought campaign, I was elected chief of the reserve in December. But as for the influence I was going to have on the country and the world, that was only the beginning.

CHAPTER FOUR

One Step at a Time

CLAIRE 1984-1994

I went to a treatment center in a town called Round Lake,
British Columbia. The program was extremely intense,
more so than I had bargained for. I had fully expected to
have to give up alcohol and drugs, but the people there wouldn't even
let me have my caffeine. They only allowed limited cigarette breaks,
which was a killer for me since I was such a heavy smoker at the time.
Coming off a 10-day drunk, this was a huge shock to my system.

I totally detoxed over the course of the first week, at which
point I went to see my counselor. I told her that I wasn't going to
be sticking with the program, that though their program was really
amazing, it wasn't for me. Upon hearing this, my counselor stood up

and pointed her finger at me. "I guarantee you'll be drunk in a week," she said. Of course, I now realize that she was desperately trying to convince me to stay.

My counselor stood up and pointed her finger at me. "I guarantee you'll be drunk in a week," she said.

For a moment, I didn't know what to say. I couldn't believe the horrible thing she had just said to me, and yet it stirred up in me the very emotions that ended up saving my life, the same emotions that had caused Larry to survive in Toronto after running away from home. I was going to prove this woman wrong, no matter the cost. I wasn't going to let her be right about me. If she didn't think I'd last a week, I would show her I could go a lifetime. As God is my witness, I stayed sober those first few months purely out of anger toward her.

That same day, I left Round Lake and hitchhiked a ride to the bus depot in nearby Vernon. From there, I rode back to Vancouver to try my hand at sobriety.

That was in August 1984, and I haven't had a drink since.

I was extremely committed to recovery, even taking time off from work to invest in therapy. I attended a lot of groups that helped me come to understand all the problems I had been born into. At the same time, I learned that I wasn't governed by them. My dependency on Alcoholics Anonymous in the first year of my recovery was actually pretty extreme. I went to more AA meetings than I can count. In Vancouver, there were 350 meetings a year, and I went to just about every single one them, sometimes taking in two or more a day. In the beginning, I didn't know how to get rid of the pain I felt inside any other way, so AA was a lifesaver. Those meetings really gave me hope for the future.

Ditching alcohol didn't automatically mean I had ditched all the other problems that were associated with it. For instance, even though I was now clean and sober, I still attracted violent men. The first guy I got into a relationship with after getting home from Round Lake turned out to be just like all the other men in my life. I naively thought that if someone could stay sober that long, they were like a god. As soon as I moved in with him, he started beating me. What struck me as such an irony was that he, too, was clean and sober ... and had been for six years. After three months, I got out of that determined to end my cycle of bad relationships.

My dependency on Alcoholics Anonymous in the first year of my recovery was... extreme. I went to more AA meetings than I can count.

As it happened, the longer I stayed sober, the better I got at sports. Having discovered my natural athleticism, I started playing more fastball. So it was that in 1985 I traveled to Victoria to participate in a provincial fastball tournament that was going on there. The tournament itself, however, turned out not to be the most memorable part of the trip. While I was there, I met yet another guy. This one I felt was different than the others. For one thing, he was gentle and very non-aggressive.

We moved in with each other within a few months, and I was in heaven. A couple years later, we got married. I really thought I had broken the pattern. Of course, we weren't entirely without conflict. The two of us were polar opposites; he wouldn't hurt a fly, and I was pretty aggressive. He didn't seem to mind, at least not at the beginning.

One of the things about the marriage I'm grateful for is that it showed me that there was a whole category of men out there that I hadn't met. Men who didn't beat their girlfriends and wives. Men who were sensitive to others and not just concerned about themselves. To be frank, men who weren't terrible. Unfortunately, the relationship fizzled as quickly as it had ignited. I can't blame the whole thing on him. We weren't married long before I went through a very troubling period of my life. The onset of our separation came when I first learned about the death of my brother Wayne.

Wayne and I had been close during the times when he was sober. We would talk recovery and about the different healing methods that were available. He was one of those people with whom you could be completely open with. I was absolutely devastated when he died, as was the rest of our family. He was so young! Only twenty-nine years old! I hadn't gone through anything quite like that, and so I didn't know how to deal with it. It was even more painful to know that he had been drinking at the time of his death.

In coping with Wayne's death, I dropped to my knees every morning and asked the age-old question: "God, where did he go?"

You might say his death brought out the believer in me. I had rejected God as a child, and even gone so far as to say he didn't exist, but in coping with Wayne's death, I dropped to my knees every morning and asked the age-old question: "God, where did he go?" My old religious baggage and beliefs were tormenting me during this difficult time. I had that conversation with God for three months — at least, it was a one-sided conversation. If God was speaking back to me, I wasn't listening.

It was one of the most despairing times of my life. At one point, I went to see a grief counselor, who asked me if I knew what my brother had believed before he died. I said I thought he had believed in Jesus. All I understood about Jesus, though, was what I had been told as a kid: everything is black and white. If you sin at all, you're going to hell. Because of those deep-rooted beliefs, I had no peace about where he had ended up. "Did he believe in Christ?" the counselor asked me. "If so, he might have had a private moment with Jesus, and you don't know that. That's between him and Jesus."

While I didn't feel like this had helped me, it did form a turning point in how I viewed God. Finally, after months of asking the same question, I became determined to get a straight answer about Wayne. "All right God, where is he? I need some peace about this." As soon as the words came out of my mouth, I had an overwhelming picture of a clear, open pasture and Wayne running through it. I could smell everything … the trees, the grass, the flowers, and the water all had indescribable life. Everything felt so alive in my senses. Perhaps at the time that was the only way the Lord could communicate with me, but in that moment I knew it was God.

As I said, my husband and I were in a downward spiral. We didn't have a solid foundation in Christ, as I know now is so vitally important, and we didn't have a clear understanding of what marriage was about, or what it demanded of each of us as individuals. We were two wounded people who had met each other at very broken points in our lives. Our relationship was like a band-aid temporarily covering over our hurts. As our marriage frayed, it became obvious that we had made a terrible mistake. We parted ways in 1990, never reconciling.

When my marriage ended, I was at the six-year point in my recovery. I started to feel like I had a handle on my sexual abuse issues, and I had gone through a lot of counseling to deal with that wound in particular. After attending every class on the topic under the sun, I decided it was time to speak with my parents about the effects the abuse had had on me. By this point, it didn't matter to me whether they spoke to me anymore. I felt that I had accepted the loss of not really having had parents and that I was more like a slave for their personal use than a daughter. I realized the likelihood of them changing was not very high. By all natural circumstances, I concluded that they were lucky we were even willing to speak to them after what they had done. I knew I had to get it out in the open to avoid being consumed by it. After all, I was aware of how hardened my heart had become. I didn't want to be bitter anymore.

I was aware of how hardened my heart had become. I didn't want to be bitter anymore.

Part of my rage was directed at the people in the community who I felt must have known about what was going on at our house but hadn't done anything to stop it. As kids, we were all total psychos, fighting with other kids and exhibiting absolutely bizarre behavior. To settle this once and for all, I made an appointment back home at the reserve to look at the CAS records to see if anyone recognized what might have been happening in our home. I flew back to Ontario and made an appointment with a social worker who was able to help me dig through the files.

Before I left Victoria, I wrote a letter to my dad, telling him that I was going to be on the reserve for a few days and the reason for my visit. Despite having advance warning, when I showed up at the house he wasn't ready to have an honest conversation. Instead, he just sat and listened to me talk while my mother stood in the doorway. "I want to talk to you about what you did to me," I began. There were no responses from either of them. When I gave him the overview of what he had done and the long-lasting effects they had inflicted on me, my mom quietly stepped out of the room. I think she was scared about what he might do. "I resent that we pretend all this stuff didn't happen when it did," I went on. "I resent that when you walk into a room, we stop talking about it. I refuse to do that anymore. I don't want to pretend anymore. I want to be honest about how sick you really are!"

I told him about the help I was getting and that he was the center of the sickness, that he was the one who was sick. That was the simplest way I could think to put it, and yet I got nothing out of him. Nothing. At the very least, I thought maybe I'd get a "Gee, Claire, I'm sorry for what I did." Instead he didn't even acknowledge that I had spoken. After a few minutes of awkward silence, he got up and walked out of the room, at which point I left.

More answers awaited me in the records the social worker had dug up. I saw how many times the suspicion of abuse had been reported. It was healing for me to see because it allowed me to forgive even more.

According to the Privacy Act in Canada, the only records I was to be permitted to view were those that specifically pertained to me. However, as I looked at the files amassed for me, I realized that I was looking at a complete history of my family's reported suspicion of abuse. The records went back to 1968, when my older sister's abuse was first noticed by community members. Somehow, seeing that my dad's crimes hadn't gone entirely unnoticed brought me some reprieve from the constant barrage of anger and bitterness that had been raging inside me for such a long time. There were reports from the public health nurse and other members of the community, folks who had been concerned about what was happening in our parent's care. It was impossible to stay angry anymore, because I realized that people had been trying to help us.

The Children's Aid Society had made several visits to my parents to confront them with the allegations. Each and every time, my dad had denied them outright. When the social workers had spoken to my mother alone, she insisted that she protected us from him. There were six visitations listed in the files I was given, and each of them read the same as the others.

It was impossible to stay angry anymore, because I realized that people had been trying to help us.

I was especially interested to read the report that was made following the incident in which my mother called to have me removed from the house. It was hard to read the things she had said about me, that I was a rotten, hostile, no-good child. It made me sad that the case worker hadn't looked at all the other reports that had been filed regarding my parents and the suspicion of abuse. If she had, she would have seen the unspoken reason behind my volatile behavior. I wasn't a psychopath as my mother had suggested. I was a victim of their abuse!

Overall, the record hunt brought me a degree of healing and closure. I was given a copy of the files in a bundle, but instead of keeping it I decided to burn them all in ceremonial style. As I watched the papers go up in flames, I realized that it wasn't them that needed to change. It was me who had to change my response to them. He was always going to have his demons lurking if he didn't get the help he needed for his sexual sickness, and she was always going to be under his spell. That was the only way I was going to be able to function in the family.

As I watched the papers go up in flames, I realized that it wasn't them that needed to change. It was me.

When I got back to the west coast, a friend of mine told me about a school in Edmonton, Alberta that specifically trained people to become social workers who specialized in addictions counseling. With my background, it seemed like a natural fit. I could easily see myself helping other people through the same kinds of problems I had come through. Even though I was still somewhat unwell emotionally, it seemed like the next step in my journey. I applied for a spot in the school, being careful to be honest in the application about where I was at in my personal life.

Six months later, I heard back from them with the news that I was accepted. My start date in the program was August 1991, so I had to make arrangements to move from Vancouver to Edmonton as soon as possible.

It was an extremely difficult time for me. Here I was, moving to Alberta after having lived on the west coast all my adult life. I had lived in Vancouver for years, and despite the ups and downs I had experienced there, I loved the city. I also had a lot of family there, which made the decision to go even more wrenching. The morning I left, my sisters were outside crying as I pulled away down the street. Maybe it's a little childish that they did that, but we were very close.

I didn't know anybody in Edmonton, a chilling thought that haunted me throughout the entire 11-hour drive. I cried and cried as I drove, talking to God and asking him to give me peace. I still wasn't calling him Jesus, just "God." Whatever I called him, though, the important thing was that after so many years, I was finally opening up to him. "I trust in you as my source," I said, "and I believe you opened this door for me, led me to this opportunity. I believe you have a reason and a purpose for me coming here. Even though I don't know anybody, and that frightens me, you're going to lay the foundation for the direction I am to take." Knowing God was with me made all the difference on that trip.

Once school started, I received a tip on a job at a Native treatment center. I didn't have my certification yet. For that matter, I also didn't have much experience working in the addictions field, other than my own commitment to recovery. So it was a long shot. I thought maybe they would at least hire me as an administrative assistant, so I started volunteering there as often as my schedule allowed. I got to know some of the counselors that were working there quite well, so when the next position came up I had an edge over the competition. Lo and behold, they gave it to me. The best part was that they paid for time off work one week a month so that I could pursue my education.

My fears that I wouldn't know anybody in Edmonton turned out to be unfounded. Not only did I have a great job and some new friends, but I also hooked up with a male friend I had met several years ago in Victoria. When I first met him, I had been in my first marriage, and now that we were both available, we started spending a lot of time together. Certainly we didn't have anything serious going on – we were both kind of a mess – but we were starting to get to know each other better.

His name was Gary, and he traveled a lot for business. When I say traveled, I don't just mean he flew across Canada. He was in charge of a purchasing department and was splitting his time between Edmonton, Hong Kong, and a few other Asian countries. Because he was sometimes gone for two or three weeks at a time, he often asked me to housesit for him.

It was during one of these periods where I was staying at his house when I got a call from my sister in Vancouver. Two of my nephews, 17- and 18-years-old respectively, had been in a terrible car accident with two other boys. Both of my sister's sons were badly injured and had to be in the hospital for a long time. I was in the middle of work and school, so it was impossible to book a flight and fly back, especially since it was unknown when there would be any improvement in their condition. I was forced to wait out the time by myself, which was difficult.

It was on a Saturday night when I had a truly spooky experience that left me rattled. First of all, I was particularly lonely that evening, wishing I was with my sisters so I could be some help to them. I was overwhelmed with sadness both for my own family as well as the community at large. During my drinking years, it was not uncommon for me to have hallucinations. I know that Larry, too, had similar experiences. They're commonly referred to as DTs, or *delirium tremens*, and occur while you're sobering up or entering into a prolonged period of abstinence from alcohol or drugs. Your body is so overdosed with alcohol or drugs that you start to see things, like crawling bugs on your skin, to cite a familiar example. I'd had plenty of DTs in my drinking years when I came off long binges, but it had been years since my last episode. Keep in mind that I was seven years clean by the time this happened, so it really came out of nowhere.

I got up and sat on the edge of the bed, and just perched there for several minutes, terrified. I didn't know what to do.

While I was house sitting for Gary, I decided to lay down for a nap. I had just dosed off when I suddenly heard loud music blaring. My eyes snapped open and I could hear a voice talking somewhere in the house. There was a lot of maniacal laughing going on, too, so loud that I could hardly think. I got so freaked out, not realizing that the voice was a hallucination. I got up and sat on the edge of the bed, and just perched there for several minutes, terrified. I didn't know what to do and considered the possibility that there was a home invader loose in the house. As I sat there, trying to decide what to do next, I remembered a verse my Sunday School teacher had taught me when I was little. *At the name of Jesus every knee should bow, of those in heaven, and of those on earth, and of those under the earth, and that every tongue should confess that Jesus Christ is Lord, to the glory of God the Father* (Philippians 2:10-11, NKJV). I couldn't remember the words verbatim, but the comfort of knowing that just speaking the name of Jesus brought the spiritual world to its knees brought me the courage I needed to face my problem head-on.

So that's what I did, exactly what the verse said. I lifted my head and spoke the name of Jesus. I don't know what I had expected to happen, but the moment I said it, all the sounds stopped. Instantly. After I was sure that the noise was completely gone, I went downstairs to search the house. I looked everywhere I could think somebody might be hiding, and there was nobody there. Even though I had been motivated by fear, this was undisputable evidence to me that not only was God real, but Jesus, too. The first thing I did was pick up the Yellow Pages and start calling churches.

Finally, I was on the right track.

By this time, I was lonely, had failed at marriage, and felt like a loser for the amount of corruption I had let in during my short life. By anyone's definition of righteousness, I was not qualified to even set foot in a church, let alone the presence of God. I think the enemy was tormenting me, trying to scare me into rejecting God further, but instead I ventured closer and started attending church for the first time as an adult.

I spoke with God all the way to the church I was going to. "Now, you know, I'm only going to believe what I experience to be true. Nothing more, and nothing less.

On my first Sunday morning, I spoke with God all the way to the church I was going to. "Now, you know, I'm only going to believe what I experience to be true. Nothing more, and nothing less ... for now." I walked into church that morning not knowing what to expect, but it turned out to be the perfect time to make my debut appearance. It was as though the pastor was speaking to me directly. I just listened intently to the whole sermon as he spoke from the Book of Joel. *So I will restore to you the years that the swarming locust has eaten, the crawling locust, the consuming locust, and the chewing locust, my great army which I sent among you. You shall eat in plenty and be satisfied, and praise the name of the Lord your God, who has dealt wondrously with you; and my people shall never be put to shame* (Joel 2:25-26, NKJV). The words resonated in my heart. No matter the shame and sin that had come before in my life, God's plan was to restore me and make things right again. I realized that I had suffered the consequences of my own poor choices as an adult, but that God was still willing to restore the brokenness and suffering that had led me to make those poor choices.

After the church service, I didn't even want to leave, but I was also a little bit worried about how I was going to get along with the other people in the church. I didn't know how to talk to Christians because I'd been bitter so long. For the first few months, I would be on my way to church when the historical anger toward the church would begin to rise in me. Thankfully, I learned not to cave into my emotion. Somehow, I knew in my spirit that I was on the right track.

As I sat in my seat and the church was starting to empty, a memory came to me from when I had still been in Vancouver. I had been married to my first husband at the time when Larry called me out of the blue and told me that he was going to be in town speaking at a conference. "I've got all these Inuit people coming with me and they're going to need a place to stay," he said. "Can you help me out by taking some of them in?" I tentatively agreed, but asked him how many people we were talking about. "Oh, just a couple," he answered. Then, of course, typical of the Indian way, eight people showed up. My brother still laughs about that today, unapologetically I should add.

The only place I had room for everybody was on the floor, but we made it work. The house was so crowded that one morning Larry and I decided to go to a restaurant for breakfast. While we waited for our food, Larry tried to share the Gospel with me, but I didn't want to listen. I was completely upfront with him about it, saying, "I'm not sure I want to serve the God you serve, Larry." He just looked at me with a question in his eyes and asked me why not. "Well," I said, "there are a lot of reasons, but … I don't have any desire to become a missionary to Africa or something." In my mind, I had linked Christianity with mission trips and a boring life. I thought that if I committed my heart to God, he was going to want me to go places against my will. It seemed logical at the time, and I know a lot of people today who still think that way. Anyway, Larry started laughing. When I asked him what was so funny, he said, "He's not like that, Claire. He's a gentleman!"

The notion that God wasn't going to move me around the globe like a pawn on a chessboard was an eye-opening revelation.

I walked away from that conversation completely confused. God's a gentleman? I couldn't believe what I was hearing. Hadn't Larry grown up in the same house I had? The notion that God wasn't going to move me around the globe like a pawn on a chessboard was an eye-opening revelation.

After reliving that conversation, I looked around the church and realized I was one of the last people there. When I stepped out into the lobby, I found myself in conversation with a woman who invited me to join a group of church members at her house for a midweek Bible study. At first, I wasn't sure if I wanted to go, but by the time the day arrived I decided to give it a shot.

As I rode to the woman's house, I had the same conversation with God I had been having for the last few days. "Remember, God, I'm only going to believe what I experience to be true." I didn't know how I was going to overcome all the historical baggage I was still lugging around, but I was beginning to believe that through God the possibility existed.

The actual Bible study turned out to be interesting, but somewhat uneventful. I managed to connect with a lot of other people from the church, but I wasn't as thunderstruck as I had been at the end of the Sunday service. That is, until the meeting started to wind down. Before the group dispersed, one of the men asked if anybody in the room had a prayer request. I was quick to respond. I told them about my work at the treatment center and went on to describe to them the confusion I was feeling about the Native culture and traditions they routinely used as part of their therapy. Because I had grown up with a lot of messed up concepts about religion, my prayer request was to receive the wisdom I needed to clarify between what was appropriate to participate in at my job and what wasn't. Most importantly, I didn't want my dad's historical Pentecostal misunderstanding of the Indian culture to rule any part of my decisions. After I finished speaking, the guy who had asked for prayer requests looked at me as though the answer to my dilemma was the most obvious thing in the world. "Truth be told," he said, "you shouldn't be working there at all. That stuff is pagan!"

I shuddered as soon as he said that, immediately recognizing it as the kind of thing my father had used to say about the traditions I had been taught in grade school. Now, almost twenty years later, I knew better. I couldn't believe how judgmental this guy was being, so my natural instincts kicked in and I let him have it. "If Christ hung out with prostitutes, which the Bible tells us he did, then he must not have been anything like you. I don't think he felt that way at all." Before I knew it, I was quoting scriptural examples from the ministry of Jesus and just generally shredding him in front of all the people at the meeting. Honestly, I surprised myself with the words and information that came out of my mouth. I hadn't been aware that I knew so much about the Bible. After the group adjourned, the guy was one of the first to leave. Obviously some of the others at the group liked what I had said to him, because a bunch of them came up to encourage me. "Right on, Claire! Way to put him in his place!" It was very surreal.

> *I surprised myself with the words and information that came out of my mouth. I hadn't been aware that I knew so much about the Bible.*

As I left, I almost made the decision not to go back to that particular church. I wasn't sure how comfortable I was with this man's comments and whether other people in the group shared the same perspective. Something about it seemed wrong. I mean, what kind of Christians were these? Ultimately, I did go back, even though the experience had sparked some of the lingering anger I still had toward the Pentecostal faith. Even though I was fighting internally about whether to go back, the new spirit within me knew exactly what to do. The following Sunday, I was strengthened yet again and my eyes started to open to the truths within the same biblical passages and scriptures I had despised since childhood. It was like a light coming on, seeing how they weaved together and spoke to my own personal struggles.

With the renewed realization that Christianity held the answers I was seeking, I sought out a Christian counselor to help me navigate through the maze of confusion I still felt lost in. I didn't want to go too far too soon, but rather take it slow and undertake a cautious exploration of Jesus. Going to Christian counseling ended up being the best thing I could have done. Over six months, I made more progress than I had thought possible.

I was able to put into perspective my dad's abuse. God gave each and every one of us a will to choose, and so his decision to violate me and my brothers and sisters hadn't had anything to do with the will of God, but instead the will of my dad. Jesus hadn't done anything to me, nor had he allowed anything to happen. Because God gave man the right and responsibility of free choice, he couldn't step in and violate my father's will. For the first time in my life, I began to experience an inner freedom.

My childhood issues weren't the only areas where the counselor helped me gain perspective. We moved on to deal with my past relationships and particularly my failed marriage. The counselor explained to me the concept of creating unions. We create all kinds of unions as we move through life, often sexual ones that profoundly affect us on physical and emotional levels. She showed me a passage in which the Lord expressed his desire for people to be restored back to purity. Because I didn't even know where to begin finding healing and restoration, she suggested that I make a list of people I had slept with out of marriage. I was horrified! A list?

What my dad had done to me was not only sexual abuse, but spiritual abuse as well.

Obviously, my inclination was to run, but I reminded myself that she hadn't steered me wrong so far. So I gave her the benefit of the doubt and began my list. She led me through a process of seeking and receiving forgiveness from the Lord. I have to admit, her method helped. I began to see how God could restore my heart back to an innocent state. After spending years of my life in secular therapy that seemed to only help me intellectually, I was finally getting somewhere. I was beginning to heal emotionally and spiritually. I realized that what my dad had done to me was not only sexual abuse, but spiritual abuse as well.

The next time I saw Gary, I sat him down and explained to him the spiritual transformation I was undergoing ... and that I couldn't sleep with him anymore. Now it was *his* turn to be horrified. "Why not?" he wanted to know. I told him that now that I was a Christian – which I hadn't told him about to this point – I just wasn't okay with it anymore. "What do you mean, you're a Christian?" he asked. "What does that have to do with sleeping with me? I still don't know what you're talking about." To help him understand, I took him through my personal journey, which had led me to the church and Christian counseling. When I got to the end of the story, he was adamant about joining me in this and wanted to know where he could sign up. He thought that if he became a Christian, too, then it would be okay again for us to sleep together again. Funny though his logic was, I could understand where he was coming from. He had been raised in a secular family, so this was all new to him.

"Well, it's not about signing up," I explained. I told him that the best way to see what I meant would be to come to church with me on Sunday. Which he did. Church became a regular activity that we did together in the following weeks. In addition to starting him on his own journey to Christ, it allowed us to grow closer. But not too close. I wouldn't let it happen. I knew that he had his own baggage to deal with and I had enough wisdom to realize how easy it would be to slip into my old patterns and make the same mistakes I had with my first husband. I encouraged him to go to a Christian counselor of his own and get the help he needed, because in my heart I was already entertaining the possibility of marriage.

By 1993, I was finished my two-year program and started looking over the horizons for some new and different career prospects. Realizing that I didn't want to stay too long at the treatment center I was at, I decided to move back to the Toronto area. I was feeling nostalgic for southern Ontario after living out west for as long as I had. Before I made the commitment to move, I took a trip there to get a lay of the land. It didn't take long to find a job at a woman's shelter in Toronto. I was excited about being closer to the reserve and getting to see members of my family I hadn't seen in a while. I knew there were some potential pitfalls in going back, but I determined that this was no more than a trial run and that if I didn't like it, there was nothing stopping me from going back. Gary and I were still friends, but we were noncommittal as far as moving forward. So, since I wasn't married and didn't have any kids, this was the time of my life to be adventurous.

When I told Gary about my decision, he seemed okay with it. His sentiments were very much, "Well, all right. We're not at a place of making any permanent decisions, so I guess it's time to move on." Nevertheless, he visited me a lot after I moved. We spoke on the phone most days, and it seemed as though we were just as close as we ever were.

Then, after four months in Toronto, I received a very business-like letter from him. It was delivered by courier to my work! When I opened the envelope, on Christmas Eve no less, I found an engagement ring inside and a letter in which he asked me to marry him. I was overjoyed and immediately prepared a return letter, saying, "You're obviously ready to sign up." I couldn't help but poke fun at him for his old ideas of what becoming a Christian really meant.

Two months later, in 1994, we tied the knot in Toronto and I moved back to Edmonton with him.

CHAPTER FIVE

Lost Potential

LARRY 1994-2003

The further I went in politics and the more successful I became, the easier it was to gloss over my personal problems and pretend they didn't exist. Unfortunately, I was still far from the perfect person I aspired to be. But the one thing I gained as I moved through life was maturity and the ability to take on new learning curves.

The more successful I became, the easier it was to gloss over my personal problems and pretend they didn't exist.

After some of the political fights I had battled, it was time now to take my rightful place at the council. In 1993, I was elected chief of my community, and I was so excited to rise to the challenge. By now, I knew the players and I knew the mindset, not to mention the history of my people, and I was ready to change the lives of the people in my community in positive and electrifying ways.

The chief before me had been a retired ex-employee with General Motors and had been living off his pension. I was the youngest chief the community had had in a long time, and certainly the first one with a young family to take care of. They paid me next to nothing in the top job because they were still operating under the old model, where the chief didn't necessarily need his salary to support himself. Here I was, working long days (sometimes 12 hours at a time!) and only making enough to put food on the table and look after my existing expenses. For the first two years, my family really suffered. For the following term, I got smart about it and demanded better compensation. If the community wanted a full-time chief, they were going to have to pay for one.

One of the things that most struck me at the beginning was the influence that the chief position carried. The possibilities of change and progress seemed endless, but a lot of work was required to really get things done. The truth is that politics, and getting to the top position, isn't about wielding power. Or at least it really shouldn't be. In Indian country, the tradition is that the chief isn't the leader of all so much as the servant of all. Unfortunately, these values are changing as our politics becomes more and more like mainstream Western society. I think viewing leadership as the ultimate act of servanthood is an integral part of the Gospel. As chief, I viewed myself as the same community member I had always been, only now burdened with a host of new responsibilities.

Because of the way the council system is set up, chiefs don't make decisions on their own. Nor should they! I could not have accomplished as much as I did in office without the invaluable team of council members I had at my side. Together with our membership, we ratified a twenty-year plan for our community. Even though I wasn't in the chief's seat that long, the projects we started in my years are things that are still being carried out and completed now. All I did was get the ball rolling.

My view of the political landscape was wider than the one afforded me by my position as chief. It was also exciting for me to see the things that were happening on a national and international level. For example, our people were, and still are, active at the United Nations!

Politicians love to play their political games, and it drives me crazy.

The thing about politics that bothers me the most today is the same thing that was so prevalent when I first got involved: game-playing. Politicians love to play their political games, and it drives me crazy. If I was going to lose an election for standing up for what I believed in, then so be it. My calling was higher than simply maintaining my position from term to term. I felt like God had put me in the position of chief in order to make a difference.

If I had to put a figure to the amount of good we got done over the next four years, including all the new roads and infrastructure, new school, modern water and sewer contracts, and the settlement of small land claims that no one had been able to settle up to that point … I would guess that we gave back somewhere in the neighborhood of $25 million. That number may seem grandiose, but I've put a lot of thought to it and it's as accurate a figure as I can determine. Despite this, the council balked at every cent I asked to get paid. Through these experiences, I started to dislike the very people God had called me to lead and minister to. I tried to protect my own heart and realize that the issue of compensation was political, not personal. Eventually, I got to the point where I was able to live off my salary as chief, but it sure wasn't easy getting there.

I attribute all the speaking and perceptive abilities I developed to my early years within the church.

I also served the national interests of the Indian people, in addition to my role as chief. Through to 1997, I was also the Deputy Grand Chief for an organization called the Association of Iroquois and Allied Indians. I traveled the country on their behalf quite extensively. I was appointed to carry such portfolios as economic development, business development, health, and education. During my time with them, I was appointed chairman of a national task force with a mandate to provide creative solutions for accessing capital for infrastructure and social development on First Nation Territories. The federal government and financial institutions also proved to be an active part of this process from the beginning. Again, I attribute all the speaking and perceptive abilities I developed to my early years within the church.

At the same time as I was chief and Deputy Grand Chief, I was pastoring a church on the Six Nations of the Grand River First Nation. My trips to the Arctic were still going strong and I was president of Harvest Field Ministries, which my mentor John Spillenaar had started years before I came around. My life was understandably hectic as I tried to juggle everything at once.

I even made a run for National Chief in 1997. It was a costly experience because I had to raise the majority of my own funds. I knew the odds of winning that position were very small, but I was eager to try. Having seen all that had been accomplished on my home reserve, I knew that increased influence would yield even greater results. I didn't win that particular election, though I did succeed in getting my name recognized on a national level. Even though it's been a while since then, I still get calls to this day from people across Canada asking me to consider running again for National Chief. So far, I haven't been interested.

In 1998, I lost my position as chief to a young up-and-coming woman who seemed desperate to win. I wasn't heartbroken about it, since I had already determined in my heart that it was time to let local politics go.

Another opportunity had presented itself as I was on my way out, so I didn't feel like there was any downtime between jobs. I was quickly appointed vice-president of the Canadian Executives Services Organization, which had done a lot of international work with groups based in Ottawa, the Canadian capital. CESO conducted a great deal of overseas work in stimulating development in third-world countries. They also had a number of regional offices across Canada that dealt with the Native community. This was the part of the organization I was most involved with.

So people started to know who I was. Shortly after I began my time with CESO, the Minister of Indian Affairs in Ottawa made a public apology to First Nations of Canada for the wrongs they had perpetrated against us through the years. Since I was recognized for my work on a community and national level, the Minister invited me to the gathering. Ultimately, I felt that the apology was pretty weak, that it didn't hold much weight. I think the leadership bodies that were represented felt the same way. I suppose at the very least it was a moral pat on the back for our people – not that we need patronizing pats on the back.

In 1999, I was recruited to run for office yet again, this time for the job of Grand Chief of the Association for Iroquois and Allied Indians, which I had previously worked for as Deputy Grand Chief. I easily won that race, thus adding to my ever-multiplying list of responsibilities.

That victory was followed by the growing realization that I could no longer continue to function in all the roles I had made for myself. And so, I reluctantly let my ministry fall by the wayside, passing my responsibilities at Harvest Field on to other people. Whether I did the right thing or the wrong thing, my main motivation was that the ministry didn't pay for itself the way my other career opportunities did. Looking back now, I probably could have done things differently to make ministry more profitable, but instead I decided to let it go. That decision is in the past, it's water under the bridge, and I'm no longer consumed about it.

As Grand Chief, I kept a close eye on the dynamics of the different regions of Canada. It was interesting for me to see how differently the First Nations functioned in the eastern and western parts of the country. It was a great learning curve to take on such a new and expansive job, and I enjoyed all the travel I was able to do.

But travel across Canada was the least of my opportunities to see the world. Pretty soon I found myself on trips to Australia, New Zealand, Mexico, and various South American nations. I even went all the way to Moscow, Russia, accompanying the Canadian prime minister as part of a group of prominent dignitaries. I enjoyed speaking with ambassadors from countries all around the world.

I couldn't believe the circles in which I was running. As a child, I couldn't have imagined the far-off and exotic places my life would take me, but I'm grateful for every single one of them.

I even went all the way to Moscow, Russia, accompanying the Canadian prime minister as part of a group of prominent dignitaries.

During my last days of serving as Grand Chief, I was recruited by a financial institution in southern California, where I live now. Although I was urged to run for re-election, I decided to take the job and move my family to the U.S. Part of my reason for doing it was because I wanted to better understand the world of business and economics. The move was a good one, but it certainly came with its own set of surprises and challenges. For instance, it was one thing to live and survive on a Canadian reservation, and another matter entirely to make ends meet in California where the culture of Keeping Up With the Joneses was so prevalent. That way of life was completely foreign to us, and for the first time we had to chart new territory through the worlds of large corporations and home mortgages.

I wanted to learn more, grow more, become something more. And yet the more I achieved, the further I got from my roots. The byproduct of leaving my ministry behind and pursuing my political aspirations as far as they could take me is that I started to go away from God. Through everything I was doing, it became easier and easier to forget where all the opportunities had come from. I wouldn't necessarily say that I was backslidden, but I was losing hold of my identity in Christ.

In 2003, life was good. The sun was definitely shining on us in California. The company I worked for was growing and flying me across the country on business, and I was meeting with tribal leaders among the American Indians, going to conventions, and learning about the gaming industry. As often seemed to happen, in the midst of good times another tragedy struck the family.

My nephew Dewey was shot on our home reservation. Though not killed, he was badly wounded and fell into a deep coma. We didn't know if he would survive, let alone wake up, so I traveled back to Ontario to be with the family and provide what support I could. My sister was in an impossible situation because the doctors were telling her that it was unlikely Dewey would ever emerge from his coma. She was faced with the decision of having to remove her own son from life support. She ended up being saved from having to make that decision, though, when Dewey passed away. It was an incredibly tragic time.

While we were back, I had the chance to reconnect with my twin brother, Garry. When I saw him, he was a complete mess. His health had deteriorated so steeply since the last time I'd seen him that I knew something was wrong with him. When I asked him how he was doing and what had been going on, he told me about how he had gotten sick and gone to the hospital to get treated. But nothing had come of it and he'd been released. It was a good story, but I took it with a grain of salt. A lot of my family members had a tendency to lie when their back was to a wall, and so I simply didn't believe him.

The part of his story that was true was that the hospital, the same one that had taken care of Dewey, had seen him and released him back onto the street. Quite frankly, they shouldn't have done so; Garry looked near-death. What I knew Garry wasn't being entirely truthful about was the reason. I suspected that he knew more about what was happening to him than he was letting on.

Many years ago, Garry had confided to me that he had been one of the boys that my father and grandfather had sexually molested as a child. He had also copped to having been molested while the two of us had lived in Toronto as teenagers, though I still don't know the details surrounding that incident. Over the years, he told me a lot of personal stories like these, but certainly those two had been the first of many such cases.

He got married in the late 70s to a woman named Mary Jane, who to this day I can only describe as uptight, and together with her had an adoptive son. His marriage didn't seem to entirely close the book, however, on his sexual issues. While the two of us were living in Detroit one summer, I remember him often disappearing for several days at a time and not knowing where he was. He wouldn't tell me, and when he finally showed up again, he would tell me a story that I couldn't quite bring myself to believe.

The next time I saw Garry, he admitted to me that he was involved in a homosexual relationship.

Everything came to a head in 1986. I was gung-ho for Jesus then, and I had led Garry to the Lord. I prayed with him one night and he started going to church and seeing positive changes happen. But just like he had in Detroit so many times, he disappeared one day, just like that. The next time I saw Garry, he admitted to me that he was involved in a homosexual relationship.

Mary Jane was extremely religious, and I can't put enough emphasis on the word *extremely*. When I wasn't a Christian yet, I thought she was deeply spiritual. The more I learned about Christianity, though, I realized just how extreme she really was. She was a wingding! Mary Jane had her suspicions about him, of course, and so she had put the fear of God into him, telling him, in no uncertain terms, that he was going straight to hell. It was all fire and brimstone, and Garry was afraid. Not afraid enough to end his side relationship, but afraid enough to keep it even more hidden.

I guess Mary Jane had finally had enough of waiting for him to get his act together, so she exposed him to the whole family. When he came out of the closet, I was devastated, as was most of the family. Now that he wasn't lying to me anymore, all his strange behavior over the years made sense for the first time. Though I didn't have sleepless nights over it, I was so dismayed to find that my twin brother, who I had shared a womb with, who I had gone through so much with, had turned to a homosexual lifestyle. It left me profoundly shaken.

When the word started spreading around the family, my brothers and sisters were insistent that we all get together and talk about it. Specifically, they felt it was important for us to talk to our parents and bring them into the discussion. The consensus was that we should have a family meeting, and since I had always been a leader and an organizer, they turned to me to help facilitate it. I agreed to help, and so it fell to me to go to my dad and tell him what we were planning and ask for him to be involved. Reluctantly, he and my mom said that they would. I could tell that they were terrified about sitting down with us and talking about this stuff. After years of avoidance, they still didn't want to publicly admit to the harm they had caused us.

Throughout all the mayhem, my dad just sat in his chair, stone-faced. He wouldn't deal with anything.

The point of the meeting was for everybody to get together and basically have an intervention. We were going to confront Garry and tell him that this behavior of his had to stop. But when the day came for everybody to get together, Garry didn't show up and the meeting instead quickly went off the rails. Before long, it became a pick-on-dad event in which everybody started venting about the trash that happened to them as children. Not that I disagreed with the notion of confronting him, but it hadn't been the plan. Mary Jane wailed and cried about the state of their marriage and just how screwed up their lives were. In the meantime, everybody's dirty laundry was being aired for what was probably the first time in many cases. Throughout all the mayhem, my dad just sat in his chair, stone-faced. He wouldn't deal with anything.

The next day, the situation went from bad to worse. I was told by other siblings that my older brother and sister both had gone to my dad and apologized for the meeting. To my surprise and horror, they pointed the finger at me, blaming me for the whole debacle. Boy, had that backfired! I had innocently organized the meeting, just as the family had asked me to, and look at the thanks I got. The meeting hadn't even been my concept. So my dad forgave them.

Forgave them? Wow! They had just put the king back on his throne. From what I know about the relationship between abusers and their victims, their apology had been motivated by the guilt and shame of what had been done to them, by the feeling that perhaps somehow they were partly to blame for it. They felt sorry for him that he had been ganged up on. In any event, I was suddenly the culprit, never mind the facts of abuse that we all knew to be true.

My attitude was very nonchalant. If they wanted to blame me, that was all right. In the end, he was the one who had raped the girls and molested the boys. He had to live with that. I wasn't taking any of the baggage. After the dust settled and all was said and done, my dad wasn't held accountable for anything that was thrown at him in the meeting. He was let off the hook.

After the dust settled and all was said and done, my dad wasn't held accountable for anything.

So by 2003, when I saw the terrible condition Garry was in, I had a pretty good idea of what might be afflicting him, despite his denials. I drove him back to the hospital and tried to have him admitted. The doctor didn't want him back, explaining that they had looked him over and hadn't found anything wrong. I just looked at the doctor incredulously. Anybody who looked at Garry could tell at a glance that there was something wrong. He was extremely ill.

Claire and I took Garry out for coffee that same day, determined to get some answers. My sister Dorothy, who's a nurse, came with us as well. He was so sick that he couldn't walk around on his own, so we put him in a wheelchair. As I pushed his chair, I was once again struck by how sad it was to see my brother this way. When we finally sat down, I just looked at him and said, "Okay, Garry, you have to come clean. The doctors are saying that they've checked you and they can't find anything, but you and I both know you're not being honest with them." He started crying right away, and I gripped his hand to lend some support. He shook his head as the tears rolled down his face and kept saying the same thing over and over again: "I can't."

We found out a few days later that Garry had AIDS. The doctors told us he had about a year to live.

But we weren't backing down. "Garry, you have to tell us the truth," Claire said. "I think that you're probably dealing with something here that has to do with your lifestyle, and if that's the case, you have to say something." After much persuading, he finally agreed to go back into the hospital and tell them everything. Dorothy went with him – by now she was firmly in mother mode – and they admitted him to run some tests. Sure enough, we found out a few days later that Garry had AIDS. The doctors told us he had about a year to live.

From that point forward, his health took a sharp decline. His body wasn't taking well to the medicine he was prescribed, which meant that he was likely going to die a lot sooner than a year. He just couldn't keep down the medicine. His body was resisting it, and he wasn't strong enough to fight the disease. Within a short time, Garry went back into the hospital for the last time – and didn't come out. On the same trip I had taken to help support my sister cope with the death of her son, I found myself also saying goodbye to my twin brother. Three months after his diagnosis, he passed away.

Sonya and I attended the funeral. I sat in the church and I cried as my eyes fell on Garry's coffin. Strangely enough, I wasn't crying because he had died. I cried because of the lost potential. Three of my brothers were now in the grave – another had passed away in 1999 much like Wayne had, in a deadly car accident while on a bender – and I had shared the Gospel with all of them. I had talked to them, told them how valuable they were and that God wasn't angry with them. I told them how great their potential was, that they could achieve absolutely anything that they could imagine for themselves, that they could escape the past and get on with the future. All of my brothers could have gone to the top because of everything they had going for them, and instead they lay in the grave. They had allowed the past to take over their lives, and they paid the price. I was brokenhearted, and in many ways I still am because many of my surviving brothers and sisters are the same way.

> ### *All of my brothers could have gone to the top because of everything they had going for them, and instead they lay in the grave.*

After the funeral, I returned to California and went on with my life, but spiritually I was stuck. I had forgotten God. I had forgotten my relationship with Christ. I wasn't back on skid row, I was too classy for that, but in my heart I had gone off track.

Just as ever, I was desperately in need of a savior.

CHAPTER SIX

Second Chances

CLAIRE 1994-2007

After Gary and I were married and returned back to Edmonton, he was offered a job in Victoria, so within three months we were back on the west coast. It was a whirlwind period of time for me as I was whisked from one part of the country to another. At the end of it, though, I was back living where I most wanted to be with the man I most wanted to be with. Still, the two of us were in for some troubles of our own. We had a bit of a rocky start, partly due to the fact that we both had really strong personalities. As aggressive as I am, I think my husband is even more so, which unsurprisingly led us into a world of conflict. Whether it was deciding how to handle our finances or determining if we wanted to have children, everything was a battleground.

As aggressive as I am, I think my husband is even more so, which unsurprisingly led us into a world of conflict.

As for the question of having kids, I soon discovered that I couldn't conceive. Upon hearing this kind of news, I think a lot of women come to face a significant crisis, but to be honest, I just felt relieved to have had the decision taken out of my hands. Maybe my upbringing had something to do with my anxiety on the subject, but I just didn't feel qualified to be a parent. That was a level of responsibility I didn't feel ready for.

So our lives as a couple didn't exactly take what I would call the normal course. I was okay with that, but Gary hadn't quite let go of the idea of a family, so we mulled over the possibility of adoption. As part of my process in exploring those options, I called Social Services to ask some questions. All I wanted was to make some inquiries and gather information, but as soon as I told them I was Native they became very interested in us and tried to persuade us further. "We really need Native parents," I was told. "We have so many Native children that need homes." Now the pressure was on for us to follow through.

We were matched with a young girl from Vancouver who needed an adoptive family to go to. She was from my mother's home reserve, which seemed to solidify our connection. Before we could go any further, though, we had to undergo an extensive background check in which the adoption agency conducted ten interviews with us. It was incredibly in-depth. By the tenth session, we both realized we had come to a turning point in the adoption process. We had been approved. If we went any further there would be no changing our minds. As we left the building that day, Gary turned to me and told me what I needed to hear: "I've come to the conclusion that I really don't want kids." I had already made peace with myself about that, so it was an important point in our relationship to know once and for all that we were on the same page. At least as far as having a kid was concerned.

My husband saw a lot of possibilities for the future that I didn't. For instance, he was interested in travel and wanted us both to take a lot of time developing successful careers. I found all of this very comforting since I hadn't put much thought to that yet. There was still a small part of me that was wondering how I would look back on this decision in my old age, of not having children. With a new focus in mind now, we moved forward without looking back. At least, not right away.

Gary and I were trying to figure out how we fit together in those early years of our marriage, but we were also figuring out how we fit into the church scene. Even though we were going to church every week, I didn't feel like we had any stability in that area. For example, Gary really liked the church we were going to at the time, but I didn't care for it at all. I had let him pick the church because I thought it was appropriate to help him grow in that area. I let him make the decision. The church was Pentecostal, but I didn't know that. It triggered all my childhood buttons and made me profoundly uncomfortable at times. It was hard for me to go there.

The two of us still didn't know how to successfully resolve issues, which was made worse by the teaching we were getting. Our pastor was telling me to submit to my husband, to take a quiet approach to our marital conflict and let Gary take his role as the head of the household. This went against everything I thought was right and natural, so I wasn't all that graceful in taking that advice. I was downright offended, and I told him so.

I tried my best to be patient and we ended up sticking around that church for six months before being blown out the door. It was the middle of summer and Gary made the miscalculation one Sunday of going to church in shorts. Huge mistake. The congregation was one of those starchy groups where the men wore suits and the women pulled their hair into buns. After the service, the pastor pulled us aside and showed us the error of our ways. "I have to admit, it's entirely inappropriate to come to church this way," he said, regarding the shorts. I was at the end of my rope and didn't want to hear another word. We asked him outright what the problem was, to which he responded with a number of scriptures from the Old Testament that seemed to prove his point.

My husband was no pushover either, and we weren't going to take this lying down. "I guess I don't have very much experience with this whole church thing," I said, "but the little I do know is that Jesus is more concerned about the condition of my heart than he is with what I'm wearing. Don't you think that?" The pastor instantly became angry. I hadn't just crossed the proverbial line; I had leaped over it. Needless to say, that Sunday marked the end of our participation with the Pentecostal denomination.

We had been married for about a year at that point and it was the beginning of our growth as a couple. One of the greatest problems we faced was that neither of us had had a healthy perception of a father figure in our lives as children. Mine had been a wolf in sheep's clothing, and his father had left when he was ten. We look back now and can see how evident this gap in our backgrounds was, but in developing ways to communicate and work together and make joint decisions, we had a hard time seeing it. We had a lot of fights and incidents over the next five years, a lot of yelling back and forth. But as much as there was for us to work out, there wasn't any abuse. He never physically touched me, and I didn't hurt him either.

Everyone was so needy and it seemed impossible to help everybody who needed it.

Larry had encouraged me over the years to stay involved with the Native community, advice that came from a wealth of experience. At his urging, I got a job as a social worker for a Native organization in Victoria. Much like for Larry, it was a real eye-opener as to the extent of the need among our people. Everyone was so needy and it seemed impossible to help everybody who needed it. I had always maintained a general understanding of Indian politics and how it worked, but I was blown away by the amount of bureaucracy and paperwork I had to wade through just to do my job. We had to jump through so many hoops to get funds for programs, it made my head spin. Even for things that I felt were pretty minor, there was a never ending pile of paper to file.

It's easy to lose yourself in that kind of red tape. After a few years on the job, I started looking past the neediness of the clients and started seeing the same qualities in my fellow social workers, the very people who were providing the help. I could see my own issues clouding my ability to think clearly, and recognized the onset of burnout.

Gary and I were still struggling in our marriage, mostly due to our trouble making important decisions. There was a lot of strain, and in the middle of it I began once again questioning my decision not to have kids. Instead of pursuing adoption again, I turned to fostering. It came out of my own emotional needs, out of my latent maternal instinct. There was also a massive need, and still remains today as far as I know, for Native parents to take in Native children – or in our case, teenagers.

It all started when I got a call through a contact at work one Friday night from the Ministry of Social Services. They had a kid that they desperately needed a temporary home for, and my name had come up as a likely candidate who might be willing to take in a teenager. I said yes out of compassion and a sincere desire to do my part. Unfortunately, saying yes just that one time was like unleashing a floodgate. Before long, there was a constant stream of kids coming in and out of the house. I justified my role as a foster mother by convincing myself I was doing it out of my need to explore parenthood. The truth is, the ministry was taking advantage of me too.

Some good did come of it, though. One of the kids that lived with us had a mother who was very sick in the hospital. She had been diagnosed with lupus and also had a bad case of rheumatoid arthritis, and so she couldn't take care of her daughter at times when she was in for treatment, which was sometimes two or three months at a time. Once of the times her daughter was with us, I got a call from the mother. She wanted me to come to the hospital to talk.

When I got there, the mother pulled the doctor into the room to explain what was going on. He told me that she had been placed on a heart transplant list. I had a sick feeling in my stomach, because I knew the situation couldn't be good. The mother was 98 pounds and hadn't been able to get her weight up. She tried to be optimistic about the news, but I could tell she was scared. More than anything else, she was worried about what would happen to her daughter if she died.

The foster kid experiment continued for ten months, at which point we had to shut the door.

When the doctor left, she started to cry. I sat with her as she opened up some more. "I know what the risks are," she told me. "I know what lies on the horizon here. I can't leave my daughter alone if I don't survive this. Who would take care of her?" She went on to ask me if I would, at the very least, help steer her in the right direction if she didn't survive the transplant. I wholeheartedly committed myself to that. Just two weeks later, she passed away. We continue to have a great relationship with that girl today. She now has two little daughters of her own and is expecting a third child.

The foster kid experiment continued for ten months, at which point we had to shut the door. The revolving door of kids was putting strain on our marriage and I realized that our marriage was not mature enough to continue fostering. We had to regroup.

Remembering the positive results that had come out of my experience with Christian counseling, I decided to give it another shot. Someone had recommended an agency called Elijah House Canada, which had been founded by a Native man and his wife. Gary and I made an appointment and ended up following through with an intense week-long therapy program that provided us with excellent information. It really seemed to help us at the time, but the effects weren't long lasting. Shortly after that, we continued on our merry way, life as usual, until the situation devolved further.

To make matters worse, Gary was fired from his job. Not only that, but he was dragged through a long and nasty court battle by the company he had worked for. He was in court for nearly two years trying to resolve the dispute. The strain of marriage and dueling careers was too much to handle, and so we finally separated in the fall of 1998.

The strain of marriage and dueling careers was too much to handle, and so we finally separated in the fall of 1998.

I was full of anger at what had happened to my second marriage. How had this happened to me again? Part of my anger came from unresolved issues in the past, and part of it came from my reaction to Gary's strong personality. I couldn't pass it all off on him, though, because that wouldn't have been fair. I was just as stubborn and proud. I really had to take a close look at my own racism toward my husband. I considered the fact that it might be historical racism, that I was once again misdirecting my feelings toward him.

By the end of the year, Gary received a job offer in Seattle. I had an offer in Vancouver, so it seemed certain that we were going to part ways for good. We were still in the throes of trying to decide if we wanted to stay married while all these factors were pulling us further apart. Ultimately, we both decided to take the jobs.

Just as with the events leading up to my first divorce, I was thrown into disarray by another violent death in the family. A second brother was killed in a car accident early in 1999. He had been at the chronic stage in his alcoholism, a stage I knew all too well. Though it had come in the form of an accident, it was really the addiction that was to blame. Seeing another brother go down this way really tore me up inside.

The year came and went, and we ushered in the year 2000 living in different cities. After commuting back and forth and struggling with all these new challenges life had thrown my way, Gary and I finally arrived at a decision regarding the future of our relationship: we wanted to make it work. We wanted to fix it! Both of us had just enough conviction that we felt the need to cut the crap, get our priorities in order, and focus on reconciliation.

> *Gary and I finally arrived at a decision regarding the future of our relationship: we wanted to make it work.*

The timing was perfect. Just as I decided to join him in Seattle, he was offered yet another position, this time in California. It was a great move for us. I finally learned to totally seek the Lord in all things, to completely surrender to him in terms of the direction he wanted me to go. Through listening to him, we settled into the new community and found a great church. Where there was only confusion and instability before, we were now standing on a firm foundation. Career-wise, I was still burned out from my work in Victoria and was looking for something easier. I asked God for a job I could do with my eyes closed until I felt well again.

Lo and behold, that's exactly what I got! I was hired at first to organize the office for a small company within a big corporation in Orange County, which quickly led to a promotion to executive assistant. A few years later, I became Director of Human Resources. I chalk that whole progression up to my commitment in Christ and turning my life over to him. I learned what it meant to get myself out of the way by asking God what it is that he would have me do. I wouldn't have gotten where I am today were it not for him. I had no family around me, no one else to lean on (except Gary, of course), and so I focused on the important things: God and strengthening ties to my husband.

I focused on the important things: God and strengthening ties to my husband.

I had a handle on life for the first time. Even through Gary losing his job nine months after the move, we still managed to stay put and make it work. Once again, we had to trust God that he could take a scary situation and turn it into gold. By making better financial decisions, Gary was able to start up his own business, a business that is still running successfully today.

Out of all my brother and sisters, what happened over the years is that each of us in our own way had to put words to our childhood pain. When Garry, Larry's twin brother, passed away, a lot of members of our family finally found ways to do that. Speaking from personal experience, when you're going through that long process, the tendency is to lash out and blame others for what you're going through. Certainly we had excellent targets for that anger – our parents. But deep down, you realize that it's you who needs to own the pain and circumstances of your life and that only you that can do anything about it.

After Garry passed away, I felt angry at the injustice of it and the treatment of people who are confused about their sexuality. Somehow, it didn't seem like he got a fair shot at life, let alone healing and restoration. I missed Garry a lot and still do today. I always thought that if he had ever chose to make a commitment to healing, he would have been a powerhouse for helping people who suffered from the same issues he did.

After being "vindicated" by my older siblings' apology for their behavior in the family meeting Larry had helped facilitate, I believe my dad thought this meant he was off the hook from ever needing to take responsibility for himself and the damaging things he done to his children. He was never held accountable for what he did. There was no justice. As a Christian, we are called to be compassionate to others, but dad never showed an ounce of remorse for the violence or sexual abuse he committed against us.

He was as sick and dysfunctional in his old age as he had when he was in his prime. Even as the last of us became adults, he would be constantly pulling inappropriate stunts. A good example of that was when my dad told me a story about a sexual escapade he'd had when I was little. He started telling me about an affair he'd had with a white woman, and how it had gone on for many years behind my mom's back. I had to stop him in his tracks, wondering why on earth he had thought he could be so boundary-less to share that story with me. I looked at him and said, "Dad, it's inappropriate for you to tell me stuff like this. I'm your daughter, not your buddy. I don't want to know about your sexual escapades and the affairs you had on my mother!" He backed off after that and never again told me anything like it, but I was struck by how brazen he was. As I've said, there was no accountability.

My dad's health started to decline in November of 2006. The start of it came when he started hallucinating regularly. He went to see a doctor and was diagnosed with having had a series of mini-strokes. This development threw the family into chaos, as any crisis did. Larry had found healing by pursuing the Christian track from day one, and

I had found it initially through the 12-step program, but the rest of the family was subject to all sorts of emotional whims. Of course, our dad's decline set in motion the unresolved pain everyone had from the past. This was confusing for me and siblings at times, to say the least.

I was back home on the reserve for a short time in late 2006, so I went to see our dad. Again, I wasn't unrealistic about fixing all the problems I'd had with him. I didn't think he was going to have a change of heart and I certainly didn't think he was going to suddenly decide to have a normal father-daughter relationship with me. None of those things were going to happen and I had already made my peace with that.

I had a longing to ask him if he understood the damage he had inflicted on our mom and his children. Had he ever come to realize that what he had done was wrong? More than anything else, that was my motivation for going back. But as I sat next to him in his room, he was in and out of reality. Instead he would sort of talk and mumble to himself, seeing things in the room that weren't there. He was pretty far gone, and I just thought, *Wow!* It was a sad time for me because I realized then and there that my dad was nearing the end, and that he was nearing it without achieving any sort of resolution with his kids.

Before I left, I reached over and took his hand in mine. "Do you know who I am?" I asked. He nodded slowly and answered, "Yeah, I know who you are." In that moment, he was a different person from the man who had raped me. He was having an innocent moment, engaging me in conversation with a sincerity I had never seen. And then, just like that, he snapped back and the old man was back. It was such a heartbreaking time for me. I left and got into my car and cried all the way back to the airport. I knew he wasn't ever coming back, that he was essentially gone. At least mentally.

The only thing worse than my parents' condition was the solution the family had come up with to take care of their needs.

My mom ended up in the hospital a short time later, in February of 2007. I flew back yet again. I expected that my dad would have worsened since November, but I wasn't prepared to deal with the reality I found him in. He had declined badly. He was at the point where he was dependent on my mom and needed constant care. Because my mom was in the hospital herself, there was nobody to look after him as he got progressively worse.

The only thing worse than my parents' condition was the solution the family had come up with to take care of their needs. Since my mom couldn't care for my dad, my sisters were coming in and doing it for her. When I saw my mom, I suggested that she not ask my sisters to care for him. Instead, I wanted her to use the community services as much as she could. How could my dad expect his daughters to look after him when he had put forth zero effort to make amends and restore the mistrust that he had created? I tried to get my mom to see that my sisters couldn't do what was being asked of them. He's the man who betrayed us and disguised himself as a servant of Jesus.

As unfair as it was, out of compassion they pitched in and helped care for him during this time – but it wasn't without consequences, both physical and emotional. It took its toll on all of them.

I left and returned to California. But, of course, the crisis about who would care for him went on without me. Soon after I left, the doctors called my siblings together and told them that it was probably time to consider putting both our parents in a nursing home. They weren't sure that my mom was going to recover. The move would have been in their own best interests, but my youngest sister opted to be their primary caregiver. I stayed in contact with my sisters, always asking what the alternatives were. Even after my mom's health improved, she complained that she couldn't take care of our dad anymore. "He wants to die at home," she told us.

In lieu of any other choice, my sisters continued alternating between taking care of him. Every aspect of his care seemed challenging. In retrospect, I suppose that's fitting, seeing as every aspect of his life was as well. My hat goes off to my sisters for having the courage, willingness, and compassion to care for him. I'm of the opinion that it's only because of their belief in Jesus that they were able to do it. Were the situation viewed from non-spiritual eyes, a rational person would probably have come to the conclusion that my parents should count themselves lucky that we even spoke to them – let alone cared for my dad in his last days.

We all wanted to make peace with him in our hearts and bring some resolution to our feelings. I could see that my mother's expectation of the family to help her take care of dad was high. My sisters were troopers about it, since he made very little effort to own what he had done to us and bring about any reconciliation.

A few days before he died ,my sister called to say, "Maybe you want to come home now." I had to decline. Shaking my head, I said, "I don't want to be there when he passes away. I've resolved in my heart many, many years ago that we have not had a father-daughter relationship, and never will. I experienced the grief and loss of a father long before this. I came through the other side by my belief in Jesus Christ."

Truthfully, I was no longer bitter or angry at my dad. I just didn't want to participate in his passing. As far as I was concerned, there was no loss for me, since he had never been a father to me and I had made peace with this a long time before. "I'll come after he passes away," I told my sister. "I'll come to the funeral and help in whatever way I need to, but I'm not coming now." Her answer to that sort of surprised me. "Wow, you're healthy!" she said. "Here we are, all falling apart. We're just a mess."

I was no longer bitter or angry at my dad. I just didn't want to participate in his passing.

My youngest sister called me a few days before my dad finally died. "Dad wants to talk to you," she said quietly. I thought to myself, *How odd is this?* I had resolved that the last two trips were the last I would see of him, and he hadn't been with it enough to respond to me in any meaningful way. I had wanted to know if he had repented, if he had owned his actions, if he had understood the consequences of those actions on us, if he knew what it meant to bring his issues to Christ. Because I still had these lingering questions, I agreed to talk to him.

When my dad was handed the phone, he was in and out of reality once again. The doctors had told us to just go with any delusions he was experiencing. As he spoke to me, he was snapping back and forth between the present and the 1950s. Finally, after he had been on the phone for a while, he was self-aware long enough to say, "I want you to know that I'm sorry for all the things I did that hurt you." I felt saddened because here he was, at the end of his life, trying to fix the damage he had done. I wondered why he hadn't done this while he was still healthy.

THE *Lie* THAT BINDS

Regardless, he was genuine. I had heard him lie and bend the truth so many times that I could tell when he was being honest. But as relieving as it was to hear the words from him, I knew I hadn't really needed an apology. "You know, Dad, I'm more interested in whether you've had that conversation with Jesus. Have you had that conversation with Jesus?"

"I have."
"Did you ask him for forgiveness for sexually violating me?"
"I did."
And then he snapped into the past again.

CHAPTER SEVEN

Divine Choices

"A man dies when he refuses to stand up and speak the truth. A man dies when he does not stand up for what is right!" When we heard this said recently, we were struck by how close to home it hit us. In fact, it's one of the biggest reasons we had for writing a book in the first place. Looking at our own family, the denial of what happened to us as children has prevented most of our siblings from moving on and starting over. How can you find healing when you're still lying to yourself? To get help and escape the pain of the past, the old saying holds fast: the only way out is through.

the denial of what happened to us as children has prevented most of our siblings from moving on and starting over.

Both of us had to seek out total transformation, and even though we went about it differently, there are certain biblical principles that are inescapable. We learned that the process of change begins with honesty, which in our view is based on repentance. Repentance literally means to change the direction you're going in and stop living in denial and rebellion, which in fact is the cause of dying on the inside. We learned that honesty opens the door to acknowledging truth, and that it takes humility to admit the real truth.

All of mankind believes in some sort of creation story. For us, the creation story was – and is – based on the Bible. The Apostle Paul, in writing to the Roman church, explained that trying to obey rules and laws would never make them good enough to receive God's favor. In fact, he said that the road to repentance is easily within reach. It's as near as our own hearts and mouths.

*That if you confess with your mouth the Lord Jesus and believe in your heart that God raised Him from the dead, you **will be saved.** For with the heart one believes unto righteousness, and with the mouth confession is made **unto salvation*** (Romans 10:9-10, NKJV, emphasis added). The reason we raise these verses stems from the religious background we came from. We were brought up with a performance mentality, and we carried that mentality into adulthood. Our Pentecostal church preached this very strongly at the time. If you really take a good look at what the Apostle Paul is saying here, you'll notice that nowhere does he even so much as mention performance. It's a non-issue. The only action that is required is belief and confession. This is a powerful and freeing truth to claim for yourself. After making this confession to God, for the first time in our lives we began to discover a possible sense of destiny. For the first time, we started to view things differently. For the first time, the world around us felt different. For the first time, we began to feel the possibility of enjoying a healthy productive life.

Anyone can move from an abusive past to a restored present.

However, the process we took of coming alive was a long one. It doesn't have to be. We know that victimization is a destructive and tumultuous process, but we also know that anyone can move from an abusive past to a restored present. There came a point when we were sick of ourselves, sick of the way we were living from having been forced into the world without proper training. When it came to relationships, sexual desires, love, and finances, we were clueless! We are still learning about these things, about spending and debt, investing and budgeting, giving and receiving ... none of these areas came naturally to us, so we had to be self-taught. Trust me when we say that was the hard way of going about it. For instance, the only relationships we knew were the ones we observed in the home, and those weren't relationships worth aspiring to. Outside of force and domination, we didn't know what normal was.

That being said, and unfortunately for us, we took those same dominant traits and applied them to every situation in the outside world, only to create heartache and hardship at almost every turn. We didn't understand that the overuse of our strengths would ultimately become our greatest weakness. To those who thought they know us, or still think they do, the truth is that the person we aspire to become is still a work in progress. Both of us have begun to understand and master these concepts, but it has taken years for us to get to where we presently are. We had to find Christ and learn to rely on him before we really saw true progress.

We had to deal with attitudes as well, attitudes that provided us with more than our fair share of emotional baggage to drag around. These attitudes stretched from our views of what constituted love and affection to our views on parenting. Even though they came from the carnal world, these attitudes and mistaken beliefs came with us into Christianity. We had to unlearn them! The thing we want people to know is that it's possible to leave them behind and embrace new attitudes and beliefs. If we could do it, anyone can.

One of the pitfalls we see over and over again with addicts who come to the church is that they have a tendency to switch addictions. Instead of getting a fresh start, they trade alcohol and drugs for church. Church fills the same need that substances did before. They knew when to raise their hands and how to pray, but when they went home, they still beat their kids and carried on with business as usual. In our view, this is what happened to our dad, and he's not unusual in that regard.

We also wrestled with the master/slave relationship we had with our parents. Because we felt like servants, we did things out of fear and felt no value outside of the hard work we did. Even when we did perform, usually we were told it wasn't good enough or that we did it wrong. We lived life under a proverbial microscope, always walking on eggshells when our dad was around. Our dad called us lazy more times than we could possibly count. He never had a good word for any of us. All we got was constant abuse, verbally, physically, and sexually.

Those words had long-reaching effects on us. The Bible tells us that life and death are in the power of the tongue (Proverbs 18:21). Each and every one of our siblings was destroyed by the words that were spoken over them. The proof of this lies in the three graves in which we buried our brothers. They had so much going for them, and yet they allowed themselves to be governed by the negativity that had been bred into them from a young age. "A word fitly spoken is like apples of gold in pictures of silver" (Proverbs 25:11). Had our grandfather, dad, or mother known this scripture, it might have somewhat altered our course in life.

> *Because of where we came from, we couldn't fathom a God that loved us. It was completely beyond our limited frames of reference.*

We also had to get over the Angry God Syndrome that plagued us. Because of where we came from, we couldn't fathom a God that loved us. It was completely beyond our limited frames of reference. We were angry about anything and everything. Very few of our church leaders told us that God was good and that he was always trying to bless us in everything we did.

Strangely enough, the traditional Indian elders had a better understanding of God's grace and mercy than most members of the Pentecostal faith we belonged to. Even though the church called them heathens, our traditional ancestors were grateful for all that the Creator had provided. The trees, the grass, the animals that roamed the earth, and the winged fowl that flew in the air were given to us by the Creator for our benefit. The elders never spoke about curses. Rather, everything was positive. The church could have learned so much from them if they had only been listening to the core message that was being presented.

We were afraid of everything. We feared God, we feared our parents, and sometimes we even feared each other. The fear factor was a tremendous challenge to overcome. We had to completely change the way we saw the world. It's amazing how personally God speaks to us through scripture. The Book of Proverbs tells us that where there is ignorance of God, the people run wild (Proverbs 29:18).

A new vision was, and still is, taking shape as we continue to put all of these things in the past. We're not sweeping them under the rug, because we believe in standing up for the truth and being honest about things. Through traumatic times and all the mountains we've had to climb, we found the resolution we were so desperately searching for our whole lives.

It's simple and easy – two words that perfectly describe the Gospel.

According to the verses quoted earlier from Romans, we don't have to give up all our sins and preferences cold turkey. In our experience, the longer we walk with God, the more we begin to conform to his standards. It hasn't been a constant struggle of willpower to get everything right because we now understand that when we surrender ourselves to the Lord, a time will come when we voluntarily give up the things that we struggle with today. You see, when you come to believe in Christ, you don't necessarily understand righteousness or the new spirit within you. It's that new righteousness that draws you in to want to live right. It's simple and easy – two words that perfectly describe the Gospel.

There's a psalm that encapsulates our feelings on the subject. *Create in me a clean heart, O God; and renew a right spirit within me* (Psalm 51:10, KJV).

We did not want to be fake Christians, for lack of a better way to say it. We didn't want to just go through the motions of church; we wanted to experience God in a real and personal way ... and God continues to honor our desire.

As we've said over and over, and our testimonies clearly prove again and again, the closer we get to God, the softer our hearts become in response to him. As our hearts soften, our stubbornness and anger fades. Our deep-rooted sorrows begin to dissipate in the presence of a God who loves us perfectly and unconditionally.

The Bible is full of powerful promises and blessings that were bestowed upon us. *"The thief cometh not, but for to steal, and to kill, and to destroy: I am come that they might have **life**, and that they might have it **more abundantly**"* (John10:10, emphasis added). God really thought of everything, didn't he? We haven't lived in our inheritance our whole lives, or even now to the degree that we could, but so much is available for those who seek him.

What Jesus accomplished at the cross on our behalf ... words fail us to even attempt to describe. The price he paid for us was so personal, so powerful, that we really don't have any basis by which to compare it. As broken as our pasts were, Jesus was inconceivably more broken on the cross as he took upon himself the sins of the world. It seems impossibly epic! It seems like too great an event to wrap our minds around. And yet, in the quietest moments, when it's just you and God, you no longer require understanding or an explanation ... in those intimate times, in communion with our father in heaven, we are filled with such a sense of righteousness and perfection that we know it to be true. Jesus died just for us, and just for you – it's a contradiction that is laid to rest when we gaze into the eyes of our creator and know that we are not so sinful to commune with him now and forever into eternity. Jesus has lifted all the barriers, removed any hindrance that might keep us apart, forgiven and forgotten our deepest and darkest faults so that we can experience him. His love never changes. It stays the same yesterday, today, and tomorrow. For people like us who came from backgrounds in which we had no stability, this is a powerful revelation.

The kingdom of heaven is ours! Even when we don't think we deserve it, Jesus is reminding us that there's nothing we can do to change God's mind about us. What better inheritance could we hope to receive?

We made deliberate choices to follow God and leave some of the details to him. We call these divine choices, and it's vitally important for you to consider making that choice for yourself. Although there are programs and communities that offer excellent information and help in overcoming our issues and moving on, the best source for healing can be found in the loving arms of our Savior. Once our identities are firmly rooted in Christ and not the addictions that plague us, we're on firm footing.

> ### *Our mission is to set the record straight: we are, all of us, sons and daughters of a loving father that desires only the best for his children.*

It's still amazing how far we've come, how God was able to take a situation that was so negative and traumatic and turn it into a ministry that is helping so many people to overcome their own destructive patterns. In our darkest moments, there was always the hope of freedom and deliverance. God is that hope, developing and sustaining us, providing an infusion of passion that is impossible to obtain from any other source.

Our experience of being raised in the Pentecostal movement turned us off completely to Christianity. We can't fault the entire Pentecostal denomination for our woes, however. Our experiences came through individuals that didn't have a clear understanding of the God they served. Our views and opinions of God were warped by misinformation from sometimes well-intentioned people, and we believe that the majority of the world is similarly confused about who God really is and what he wants for us. Our mission is to set the record straight: we are, all of us, sons and daughters of a loving father that desires only the best for his children.

The Lie That Binds

There is never a quick fix that will resolve the damage that has so deeply affected us on the inside. The sad part is that many look for the cheap way to fix their problems, all the while missing the path that leads to real life. We need only to allow time to be the judge of the path we choose.

The lie that binds will forever keep us in bondage until we make a choice to travel the good road and make amends where we can. Forgiveness is the beginning of that good road. When we ask forgiveness for the violations we have instilled on others and ourselves, we clear the path in our hearts to begin a fresh journey.

Your own personal divine choice is never more than a few moments away.

That being said, there are some that we have knowingly and unknowingly wronged and hurt over the years while we were on this journey. Some of you may be in the distant past while some may be more recent. Whatever the case, we take this opportunity to say that we're truly sorry for allowing our emotions to rule our choices, and more so for participating in acts that only lead to destruction. If you are one that either of us has inflicted pain upon, we ask your forgiveness and hope that you will release us of the harm we may have caused, in whatever form that it came.

Through God, there is hope for tomorrow. But don't just take our word for it … try it for yourself today. Your own personal divine choice is never more than a few moments away. If you have read this book and something has struck a nerve in you, it is our hope that, through reading our real life stories, you will take a chance, get the weight off your shoulders, and experience what it's like to truly breathe a nice, long sigh of relief. You can begin to see today that your future is now.

ABOUT THE AUTHORS

Larry Sault came from a dysfunctional, destructive lifestyle that caused much pain, anger, and bitterness in his life. After getting saved in 1981, Larry devoted himself to the ministry, traveling through the Canadian Arctic, where he spent more than 15 years raising leaders, building churches, hosting major conferences, and developing short-term bible schools. He has also brought his influence to bear on Indian politics, serving as Chief of his home reservation for four years. He was also elected Grand Chief of the Association of Iroquois and Allied Indians, gaining regional, national, and international exposure. His ministerial and political endeavors have taken him around the world where he has spoken at prestigious universities, corporate functions, and leadership seminars. Today, Larry owns his own business and travels extensively across the country.

Claire Heath has committed her adult life to serving the Lord by carrying his message of hope and healing to those in need. Claire is one of the founders of *Divine Choices*, a ministry and non-profit organization that helps people who have suffered from the debilitating affects of sexual abuse. Thanks to 24 years of recovery and the saving grace of God, Claire's own success story exemplifies the *Divine Choices* model that she prays will empower others to experience the full restoration of Jesus Christ. As a visionary leader and coach, Claire has years of experience in social work, substance abuse treatment, and human resource management. She is currently the Director of Human Resources with Dealtree Inc.

PERSONAL NOTES

THE *Lie* THAT BINDS

Personal Notes

THE *Lie* THAT BINDS